Copyright © 2024 by Jonathan T. Morgan (Author)
All rights reserved. This book or any portion thereof may not be reproduced or used in any manner whatsoever without the express written permission of the publisher except for the use of brief quotations in a book review.

This book is copyright protected. This is only for personal use. You cannot amend, distributor, sell, use, quote or paraphrase any part or the content within this book without the consent of the author. Please note the information contained within this document is for educational and entertainment purposes only. Every attempt has been made to provide accurate, up to date and reliable complete information. No warranties of any kind are expressed or implied.

Readers acknowledge that the author is not engaging in the rendering of legal, financial, medical or professional advice. The content of this book has been derived from various sources. Please consult a licensed professional before attempting any techniques outlined in this book.

By reading this document, the readers agree that under no circumstances are the author responsible for any losses, direct or indirect, which are incurred as a result of the use of information contained within this document, including but not limited to errors, omissions or inaccuracies.

Thank you very much for reading this book.

Title: Ripple's Roadmap: How Digital Assets Will Transform Cross-Border Payments
Subtitle: A Vision for Faster, Efficient Worldwide Financial Flows

Series: Bridging Borders: XRP's Vision for Faster, Efficient Worldwide Transactions: Ripple's Mission to Revolutionize Payments through Blockchain Innovation
Author: Jonathan T. Morgan

Table of Contents

Introduction 5
The origins of Ripple 5
Company mission and values 7
The Role of XRP 10

Chapter 1: RippleNet - A Network of Networks 13
Connecting Payment Providers Globally 13
Standardized Technology and Rules 19
Real-Time Settlement Between Endpoints 24
Use Cases Across Verticals 30

Chapter 2: xRapid - Leveraging XRP for Liquidity 37
On-Demand Liquidity Between Currencies 37
Faster Access to Emerging Market Corridors 43
XRP Minimized Costs and Unlocked Capital 50
Partner Financial Institutions 57

Chapter 3: xCurrent - Interledger for Payment Tracking 66
Send Payment Info and End-to-End Tracking 66
No Need to Move Funds Between Ledgers 72
Integrates with Legacy Systems 80
Provides Transparency into Global Payments 87

Chapter 4: xVia - A Standard API for Payments 94
Single Connection to Payment Providers Globally 94
Abstraction Layer over RippleNet 101
Easy Integration for Business Applications 108
Reduces Need for Manual Reconciliation 115

Chapter 5: Use Cases - RippleNet in the Real World 122
Santander Bank Implementation for Retail Customers 122
MoneyGram Using xRapid for Cheaper Remittances 129
MercuryFX: Transferring Payments in Minutes 135
Cuallix: Opening New Markets with XRP 141

Chapter 6: Beyond Payments - Smart Contracts and NFTs **146**
Ability to Represent Any Asset on Ledger................................... *146*
Issuing, Trading, and Redeeming Tokenized Assets................... *151*
Programmable Swaps, Loans, and Escrows............................... *156*
New Economies Built on Decentralized Finance *161*
Chapter 7: The Future with the Internet of Value **165**
Internet-Connected World but Not Value *165*
RippleNet as the Foundational Internet of Value Network *172*
True Real-Time Settlement between Ledgers *178*
Applications We Can't Yet Envision *184*
Conclusion **188**
Key Innovations of RippleNet and XRP.. *188*
Continuing to Evolve and Expand.. *196*
Roadmap to the Future of Value Transfer *200*
Glossary..**205**
Potential References **208**

Introduction
The origins of Ripple

In the fast-evolving landscape of global finance, the need for seamless and efficient cross-border payments has never been more pronounced. Traditional banking systems have grappled with the challenges of speed, cost, and transparency, leaving a gap that pioneering technologies seek to fill. At the forefront of this transformative wave is Ripple, a company with a vision to revolutionize the way money moves across borders. To embark on the journey of understanding Ripple's pivotal role in the future of payments, it is essential to trace back to its origins.

The Origins of Ripple

The roots of Ripple can be traced back to the year 2004 when a computer programmer named Ryan Fugger envisioned a decentralized monetary system through a platform called RipplePay. Fugger's idea centered around the concept of trust networks – a web of trust where individuals could extend credit to one another. While the idea was groundbreaking, it wasn't until 2012 that Chris Larsen and Jed McCaleb reimagined and expanded upon Fugger's vision.

Chris Larsen, a seasoned entrepreneur with a background in financial services, and Jed McCaleb, the co-founder of the infamous Mt. Gox exchange, joined forces to create OpenCoin. This company would later evolve into what we now know as Ripple Labs. Their goal was clear: to develop a technology that could facilitate secure, instant, and cost-effective international money transfers.

The Ripple protocol, as we know it today, was officially released in 2012, laying the foundation for a decentralized digital payment protocol that could facilitate real-time, cross-border transactions. The protocol aimed to address the inherent flaws in traditional banking systems – delays, exorbitant fees, and the lack of interoperability between different financial institutions.

Ripple's journey gained momentum in 2013 when it attracted investment from notable venture capital firms, including Andreessen Horowitz and Google Ventures. This financial backing allowed Ripple to further refine its technology and expand its reach within the financial industry. The company's commitment to solving real-world problems in the global financial system positioned it as a trailblazer in the realm of digital payments.

As Ripple continued to gain recognition and partnerships, its commitment to innovation led to the creation of RippleNet, a decentralized network that aimed to connect financial institutions worldwide. RippleNet served as the infrastructure for a new era of financial transactions, where speed, security, and transparency were not compromised.

In the subsequent sections of this exploration, we will delve into the intricacies of Ripple's offerings, particularly focusing on the role of XRP, the digital asset native to the RippleNet ecosystem. Before we embark on this journey, it is crucial to appreciate the company's humble beginnings, rooted in the vision of a decentralized, trust-based monetary system. Ripple's evolution from a concept on a computer programmer's screen to a global player in the financial technology sector is a testament to the power of innovation and the pursuit of a more interconnected and efficient world of finance.

Company mission and values

As we embark on a journey to unravel the future of cross-border payments through the lens of Ripple and its digital asset XRP, it's imperative to delve into the core principles that guide the company. Beyond technological innovation, Ripple's mission and values serve as the compass navigating its trajectory in the complex world of global finance.

Company Mission and Values

At the heart of Ripple's endeavors is a mission that transcends mere financial transactions. The company envisions a world where money moves as seamlessly as information, empowering individuals and businesses across borders. Ripple's mission is rooted in the belief that a more connected and accessible financial system can pave the way for widespread economic empowerment.

Central to Ripple's mission is the commitment to enabling the Internet of Value – a concept that envisions a world where the transfer of value, much like the exchange of information on the internet, is instant, secure, and globally accessible. The Internet of Value is not just a technological ambition for Ripple; it represents a fundamental shift in the way society perceives and utilizes financial transactions.

Ripple's mission extends beyond facilitating cross-border payments. It aspires to create an inclusive financial ecosystem where every individual, regardless of their geographical location or economic status, has access to efficient and affordable financial services. This mission aligns with the broader global initiative to address financial inclusion, where traditional banking systems have often fallen short.

Complementing Ripple's mission are the values that guide the company's day-to-day operations and decision-making processes. Transparency stands as a foundational principle, reflecting Ripple's commitment to fostering trust within the financial ecosystem. In an industry where opacity has been a historical challenge, Ripple places a premium on providing clear and unambiguous information to its partners, clients, and the broader community.

Integrity is another core value that permeates Ripple's corporate culture. As the company navigates the complex landscape of financial technology, maintaining the highest standards of integrity is non-negotiable. Ripple recognizes that trust is a currency of its own, and without it, the vision of a seamless, global financial network cannot be realized.

Innovation is deeply ingrained in Ripple's DNA. The company views technology not merely as a tool but as a catalyst for positive change. Ripple continuously seeks innovative solutions to address the pain points of traditional banking systems. Whether through the development of cutting-edge protocols or the exploration of new use cases for digital assets, innovation remains a driving force propelling Ripple toward its vision of a more connected world.

Collaboration is a key pillar supporting Ripple's mission. Recognizing the complexity of the financial ecosystem, Ripple actively seeks partnerships with financial institutions, regulatory bodies, and technology providers. The company understands that achieving its goals requires a collective effort, and collaboration is essential for building a robust and inclusive financial infrastructure.

Security is paramount in the world of digital finance, and Ripple places a steadfast emphasis on safeguarding its technology and the assets of its users. In an era where cybersecurity threats loom large, Ripple's commitment to implementing robust security measures underscores its dedication to protecting the integrity of the global financial system.

Ripple's mission and values form the bedrock upon which the company stands as it navigates the dynamic landscape of cross-border payments and digital assets. The chapters that follow will illuminate how these principles manifest in Ripple's key offerings, particularly focusing on the role of XRP in transforming the traditional paradigms of global financial transactions. By understanding Ripple's mission and values, we gain insight into the driving force behind the technological innovations that are reshaping the future of payments.

The Role of XRP

As we embark on a voyage into the future of cross-border payments through the lens of Ripple, it is imperative to cast a spotlight on the linchpin of this transformation – the digital asset known as XRP. Ripple's innovative approach to global finance is not solely encapsulated in its technological solutions but is profoundly intertwined with the role that XRP plays within the RippleNet ecosystem. To comprehend the true essence of Ripple's vision, it is essential to explore the multifaceted role that XRP assumes in revolutionizing the traditional dynamics of cross-border transactions.

XRP as a Bridge Currency:

At the core of XRP's role within Ripple's ecosystem is its function as a bridge currency. In traditional cross-border transactions, the absence of a universal intermediary often leads to a cumbersome process involving multiple currency conversions. XRP emerges as a solution to this challenge by serving as a bridge between different fiat currencies. Its inherent design, with a focus on speed and liquidity, positions XRP as an ideal intermediary asset for facilitating seamless transactions across borders.

The utilization of XRP as a bridge currency introduces a crucial element of efficiency into the global financial system. Unlike traditional correspondent banking, where transactions may involve multiple intermediaries and take days to settle, XRP enables near-instantaneous settlement. This rapid settlement capability not only reduces transaction times but also minimizes exposure to volatility, offering a level of predictability often absent in traditional cross-border transactions.

XRP and On-Demand Liquidity (ODL):

Ripple's commitment to efficiency and cost-effectiveness is epitomized by its on-demand liquidity (ODL) solution, which leverages XRP as a bridge asset. ODL represents a paradigm shift in the world of remittances and cross-border payments, addressing the challenges associated with pre-funding and liquidity management.

Traditionally, financial institutions engaged in cross-border transactions needed to pre-fund accounts in destination countries to facilitate timely settlements. This tied up significant capital and exposed institutions to liquidity risks. With ODL, powered by XRP, the need for pre-funding is obviated. Instead, XRP serves as the intermediary, allowing for real-time conversion and settlement, minimizing the capital locked in pre-funded accounts.

XRP's Liquidity Benefits:

The liquidity profile of XRP further enhances its role in transforming cross-border payments. Ripple's vision has always been to provide financial institutions with a reliable and liquid bridge currency, and XRP fulfills this role admirably. Its design ensures that transactions, regardless of the magnitude, can be executed swiftly and with minimal impact on market prices.

The liquidity benefits of XRP are particularly pronounced in corridors where access to traditional banking infrastructure is limited. By enabling instantaneous transactions and reducing the reliance on pre-funded accounts, XRP opens up new possibilities for financial inclusion. This is exemplified in the realm of remittances, where individuals, especially in emerging markets, stand to benefit from faster, more affordable cross-border transactions.

XRP's Role in Cost Reduction:

A central tenet of Ripple's mission is to alleviate the inefficiencies and high costs associated with cross-border payments. XRP plays a pivotal role in achieving this objective by significantly reducing transaction costs for financial institutions. The speed and efficiency inherent in XRP-powered transactions translate to lower operational costs and, subsequently, more competitive pricing for end-users.

In corridors where pre-funding requirements have traditionally inflated costs, XRP's on-demand liquidity model delivers tangible savings. Financial institutions can redirect capital that would otherwise be tied up in pre-funded accounts toward more productive uses, fostering a more efficient allocation of resources within the global financial ecosystem.

XRP as a Catalyst for Innovation:

Beyond its role in facilitating cross-border payments, XRP serves as a catalyst for broader innovation within the financial sector. Ripple's commitment to exploring new use cases for XRP extends into realms such as decentralized finance (DeFi), smart contracts, and non-fungible tokens (NFTs). The versatility of XRP as a digital asset capable of representing any value on the ledger positions it at the forefront of the evolving landscape of financial technologies.

In the subsequent chapters, we will delve deeper into these innovative use cases, exploring how XRP transcends its role as a bridge currency to underpin a more inclusive and interconnected financial future. The dynamic and adaptive nature of XRP aligns seamlessly with Ripple's broader vision, emphasizing not only its current pivotal role in cross-border payments but also its potential to shape the financial landscape in ways yet to be fully realized.

Chapter 1: RippleNet - A Network of Networks Connecting Payment Providers Globally

In the ever-evolving landscape of global finance, the ability to seamlessly connect payment providers across borders is a cornerstone of Ripple's transformative vision. RippleNet, Ripple's decentralized network of financial institutions, stands as a testament to the company's commitment to creating a more interconnected and efficient global financial system. This chapter explores the intricacies of RippleNet, focusing on how it facilitates the seamless connection of payment providers on a global scale.

The Imperative of Global Connectivity:

At the heart of Ripple's mission lies the recognition that the challenges in cross-border payments are inherently rooted in the lack of a unified and efficient network connecting payment providers worldwide. Traditional systems, characterized by a fragmented landscape of correspondent banking relationships, often result in slow, costly, and opaque transactions.

RippleNet addresses this imperative for global connectivity by offering a standardized and secure framework that enables financial institutions to communicate and transact seamlessly. By providing a common language and set of rules, RippleNet transcends the limitations of traditional banking silos, fostering a network where payment providers, regardless of their geographical location or size, can collaborate seamlessly.

The RippleNet Architecture:

RippleNet is designed as a distributed network that leverages the power of blockchain technology. Unlike traditional centralized systems, RippleNet operates on a decentralized architecture, ensuring resilience, transparency, and security. At its core, RippleNet comprises a series of independent nodes – the network participants – each contributing to the strength and efficiency of the overall network.

The architecture of RippleNet is modular, allowing financial institutions to adopt specific Ripple solutions based on their unique needs. The three primary solutions within RippleNet – xCurrent, xRapid, and xVia – offer varying degrees of functionality, from real-time payment tracking to on-demand liquidity leveraging the digital asset XRP.

Seamless Integration with Existing Infrastructure:

One of the key strengths of RippleNet is its compatibility with existing banking infrastructure. Recognizing the diverse technological landscapes of financial institutions globally, Ripple has ensured that its solutions seamlessly integrate with legacy systems. This compatibility minimizes disruptions during the adoption process, allowing financial institutions to harness the benefits of RippleNet without overhauling their entire infrastructure.

Through standard Application Programming Interfaces (APIs) and adherence to international payment standards, RippleNet facilitates a smooth and efficient integration process. This interoperability is a crucial factor in Ripple's strategy to bring together payment providers from various corners of the globe, fostering a network that transcends the limitations of traditional borders.

Realizing the Vision of a "Network of Networks":

The concept of a "Network of Networks" encapsulates Ripple's vision for RippleNet – a global framework where individual financial networks seamlessly interconnect. Ripple envisions a future where disparate payment providers, banks, and financial institutions are not isolated entities but integral participants in a unified, global network.

This interconnected ecosystem eliminates the need for multiple intermediaries in cross-border transactions. Instead of relying on a web of correspondent banking relationships, payment providers within RippleNet can communicate directly, reducing friction, cutting costs, and accelerating transaction times. The result is a financial landscape characterized by efficiency, transparency, and a significant reduction in counterparty risk.

Benefits for Payment Providers:

For payment providers entering the RippleNet ecosystem, the benefits are multifaceted. One of the primary advantages lies in the enhanced speed of transactions. RippleNet's decentralized architecture and utilization of blockchain technology enable real-time settlement, a stark contrast to the delays associated with traditional correspondent banking.

Cost reduction is another compelling advantage for payment providers. The streamlined nature of RippleNet transactions, coupled with the elimination of the need for multiple intermediaries, leads to lower operational costs. Financial institutions can allocate resources more efficiently, redirecting capital that would otherwise be tied up in pre-funded accounts toward more strategic initiatives.

Transparency is a critical aspect of RippleNet, providing payment providers with a level of visibility into the entire transaction lifecycle that was previously unattainable. The decentralized nature of the network ensures that information is securely and transparently shared among participants, fostering trust and accountability.

Global Reach and Financial Inclusion:

RippleNet's prowess in connecting payment providers globally extends beyond established financial institutions to reach underserved regions. In many parts of the world, access to efficient cross-border payment solutions is limited, leading to financial exclusion. RippleNet, with its focus on inclusivity, opens new possibilities for financial institutions in these regions to connect with the global economy.

Emerging markets, in particular, stand to benefit significantly from the global connectivity offered by RippleNet. By providing a platform where financial institutions from diverse backgrounds can transact seamlessly, Ripple facilitates economic growth, empowers individuals and businesses, and contributes to a more inclusive global financial ecosystem.

Case Studies:

To illustrate the practical impact of connecting payment providers globally through RippleNet, we turn our attention to real-world case studies. Financial institutions around the world have embraced RippleNet to overcome the challenges of traditional cross-border payments. Institutions like Santander, Standard Chartered, and SBI Holdings have leveraged RippleNet to enhance the speed, efficiency, and transparency of their international transactions.

Santander, for instance, implemented RippleNet to offer its retail customers in select regions a faster and more cost-effective cross-border payment solution. The seamless integration with RippleNet allowed Santander to provide real-time settlement for its customers, enhancing their overall banking experience.

Standard Chartered, a global banking giant, adopted RippleNet to bolster its corporate and institutional banking services. The network's ability to facilitate real-time settlement and provide end-to-end visibility into transactions resonated with Standard Chartered's commitment to delivering innovative and efficient financial solutions.

SBI Holdings, a financial conglomerate based in Japan, forged strategic partnerships with Ripple to enhance its remittance services. By incorporating RippleNet into its operations, SBI Holdings achieved faster and more cost-effective remittances, catering to the evolving needs of its customer base.

These case studies underscore how connecting payment providers globally through RippleNet translates theory into tangible, impactful outcomes for financial institutions and their clients. The success stories highlight the network's ability to address the diverse needs of institutions, irrespective of their size or geographical location.

Challenges and Considerations:

While the benefits of connecting payment providers globally through RippleNet are evident, it is essential to acknowledge the challenges and considerations inherent in this transformative process. Regulatory compliance, for instance, poses an ongoing consideration for financial institutions entering the RippleNet ecosystem. The evolving landscape of digital assets and blockchain technology demands a nuanced approach to compliance, and financial institutions must navigate regulatory frameworks to ensure a smooth and compliant integration with RippleNet.

Interoperability with other networks is another consideration, especially as the global financial landscape continues to witness the emergence of various blockchain-based solutions. Ensuring seamless communication and collaboration between different networks is crucial for RippleNet to realize its potential as a "Network of Networks."

Additionally, the education and adoption curve plays a significant role in the global connectivity envisioned by RippleNet. Financial institutions may encounter resistance or skepticism as they transition from traditional systems to decentralized networks. Addressing these concerns requires a concerted effort to educate stakeholders, showcase successful implementations, and demonstrate the tangible benefits of embracing RippleNet.

In conclusion, connecting payment providers globally through RippleNet represents a pivotal step toward reshaping the future of cross-border payments. The network's architecture, interoperability, and commitment to inclusivity position it as a transformative force in the global financial landscape. The next chapters will delve deeper into specific components of RippleNet, exploring how standardized technology and rules, real-time settlement, and diverse use cases contribute to the network's overarching goal of revolutionizing cross-border payments.

Standardized Technology and Rules

In the intricate landscape of cross-border payments, where diverse financial institutions and systems converge, the need for standardized technology and rules is paramount. RippleNet, Ripple's revolutionary decentralized network, addresses this imperative by introducing a standardized framework that not only facilitates seamless communication but also ensures adherence to a set of universal rules. This chapter delves into the intricacies of how RippleNet's standardized technology and rules lay the foundation for transforming the traditional dynamics of cross-border transactions.

The Challenge of Fragmented Systems:

The traditional cross-border payment landscape has long been plagued by a lack of standardization. Financial institutions operate on disparate systems, each with its own set of rules, protocols, and technologies. This fragmentation gives rise to inefficiencies, delays, and a lack of interoperability, hindering the seamless flow of value across borders.

RippleNet steps into this complex ecosystem with a vision to create a uniform and interoperable network that transcends the limitations of traditional silos. Standardized technology and rules form the linchpin of this vision, providing the essential framework for financial institutions to connect, communicate, and transact on a global scale.

The Ripple Protocol Consensus Algorithm:

At the heart of RippleNet's standardized technology is the Ripple Protocol Consensus Algorithm (RPCA). Unlike traditional proof-of-work algorithms used in many blockchain systems, RPCA is designed for efficiency, scalability, and environmental sustainability. It enables consensus across the distributed network of RippleNet nodes, ensuring that all participants agree on the state of the network.

The RPCA mechanism allows RippleNet to achieve consensus on the order and validity of transactions in a matter of seconds. This speed is crucial for real-time settlement, a key differentiator that sets RippleNet apart from traditional systems that often involve days of waiting for transactions to clear.

Interledger Protocol (ILP) for Seamless Interoperability:

In addition to RPCA, RippleNet leverages the Interledger Protocol (ILP) to enhance interoperability between different ledgers and networks. ILP serves as an open protocol for connecting disparate payment networks, allowing value to flow seamlessly across them. This interoperability is a fundamental aspect of RippleNet's commitment to creating a "Network of Networks."

ILP achieves this interoperability by providing a standardized way for ledgers to communicate and settle transactions. Whether a financial institution is using a traditional banking ledger, a blockchain-based ledger, or any other form of digital ledger, ILP ensures a common language for value transfer. This eliminates the need for complex integrations and fosters a more inclusive and interconnected global financial ecosystem.

Consistency in Transaction Finality:

Standardized rules within RippleNet extend to the concept of transaction finality. In traditional banking systems, the finality of a transaction often involves multiple steps, leading to delays and uncertainties. RippleNet, on the other hand, ensures rapid and consistent transaction finality through its consensus algorithm.

Once a transaction is validated by the network through the consensus process, it is considered final. This consistency in transaction finality not only accelerates settlement times but also provides a level of predictability and transparency that is crucial for financial institutions and their clients.

Smart Contracts on RippleNet:

The standardized technology of RippleNet also extends to the realm of smart contracts. While smart contracts have gained prominence in blockchain ecosystems, RippleNet integrates them seamlessly, offering additional layers of functionality to its participants.

Smart contracts on RippleNet are programmable and can be executed automatically based on predefined conditions. This feature opens up a myriad of possibilities for automation within the network, reducing the need for manual interventions and streamlining complex processes. Whether it's automating compliance checks, triggering conditional payments, or implementing sophisticated financial instruments, smart contracts enhance the efficiency and flexibility of RippleNet.

Rules Governing Participant Behavior:

In addition to technological standards, RippleNet establishes a set of rules governing participant behavior within the network. These rules, often referred to as the Ripple Protocol Rules, ensure that all participants adhere to a common set of principles. This includes rules related to transaction format, data integrity, and the prevention of malicious activities.

The adherence to standardized rules not only fosters a sense of trust among network participants but also contributes to the security and stability of the overall network. Financial institutions entering RippleNet can be confident that their counterparts across the globe operate within a well-defined and secure framework.

Benefits of Standardization:

The standardization of technology and rules within RippleNet yields a multitude of benefits for its participants. One of the primary advantages is the ease of integration. Financial institutions can seamlessly connect to RippleNet without the need for extensive customizations or complex integrations. This simplifies the onboarding process, enabling institutions of varying sizes and technological capabilities to harness the power of RippleNet.

Standardization also contributes to the network's efficiency. The common language established by ILP, the consensus achieved through RPCA, and the adherence to protocol rules ensure that transactions occur smoothly and swiftly. This efficiency is particularly crucial in the context of cross-border payments, where delays and uncertainties have traditionally been pervasive.

The predictability and transparency afforded by standardized technology and rules translate into enhanced trust among network participants. Financial institutions can engage in cross-border transactions with a higher degree of confidence, knowing that the network operates on a consistent set of principles. This trust factor is foundational to Ripple's vision of creating a global financial network that fosters collaboration and inclusivity.

Global Regulatory Compliance:

The standardized technology and rules within RippleNet also play a pivotal role in addressing regulatory compliance. In the dynamic landscape of digital finance, regulatory frameworks vary significantly from one jurisdiction to another. RippleNet's commitment to adhering to international payment standards and protocols ensures that participants can navigate regulatory requirements with confidence.

By establishing a secure and standardized environment, RippleNet provides financial institutions with the tools and frameworks needed to meet regulatory obligations. This is particularly critical as regulators globally are grappling with the implications of digital assets and blockchain technology. RippleNet's proactive approach to compliance positions it as a responsible participant in the broader financial ecosystem.

Challenges and Considerations:

While the benefits of standardized technology and rules within RippleNet are evident, challenges and considerations exist. One notable challenge is the evolving nature of regulatory frameworks. As governments worldwide adapt to the emergence of digital assets and decentralized networks, financial institutions must stay abreast of regulatory developments and ensure ongoing compliance.

Interoperability with existing financial systems is another consideration. While RippleNet's standardized technology is designed for seamless integration, the diverse technological landscapes of financial institutions globally present unique challenges. Institutions must carefully plan and execute their integration strategies to ensure compatibility with existing infrastructures.

Educating stakeholders about the benefits and implications of standardized technology and rules is a crucial aspect of overcoming resistance or skepticism. Financial institutions may encounter internal or external stakeholders who are unfamiliar with the nuances of decentralized networks. Clear communication and educational efforts are essential to facilitate a smooth transition into the RippleNet ecosystem.

In conclusion, the standardization of technology and rules within RippleNet serves as the bedrock of its transformative impact on cross-border payments. The Ripple Protocol Consensus Algorithm, Interledger Protocol, and smart contract capabilities establish a robust foundation, enabling financial institutions to transact seamlessly on a global scale. As we progress through subsequent chapters, we will explore how real-time settlement and diverse use cases further contribute to RippleNet's overarching goal of revolutionizing cross-border transactions.

Real-Time Settlement Between Endpoints

In the realm of cross-border payments, the concept of real-time settlement represents a paradigm shift from the traditional banking systems where transactions often took days to clear. RippleNet, Ripple's decentralized network, stands at the forefront of this transformation by introducing real-time settlement between endpoints. This chapter delves into the significance of real-time settlement within RippleNet, exploring how it revolutionizes the speed, efficiency, and dynamics of cross-border transactions.

The Need for Real-Time Settlement:

Traditional cross-border payments have long been characterized by extended settlement times, often attributed to the complex web of correspondent banking relationships and the reliance on outdated systems. Financial institutions engaged in cross-border transactions typically faced delays ranging from several days to weeks, exposing them to currency volatility and counterparty risks.

Real-time settlement addresses this inherent challenge by enabling the immediate and irreversible transfer of value between parties. In the context of RippleNet, real-time settlement becomes a cornerstone feature, offering financial institutions a level of speed and certainty previously unattainable in the traditional cross-border payment landscape.

The Ripple Protocol Consensus Algorithm (RPCA):

At the heart of real-time settlement within RippleNet lies the Ripple Protocol Consensus Algorithm (RPCA). Unlike the energy-intensive proof-of-work mechanisms employed by some blockchain networks, RPCA is designed for efficiency and speed. It facilitates consensus among the distributed network of RippleNet nodes, ensuring that all participants agree on the validity and order of transactions in a matter of seconds.

RPCA eliminates the need for the protracted confirmation times associated with traditional banking systems. Once a transaction is initiated, the network swiftly reaches consensus, and the settlement becomes final. This efficiency is not only a technological feat but a fundamental shift in the temporal dynamics of cross-border transactions.

Immediate Transaction Finality:

Real-time settlement within RippleNet translates into immediate transaction finality. Once a transaction is confirmed through the consensus process, it is considered final and irreversible. This stands in stark contrast to traditional systems, where finality often involves multiple steps and can be subject to delays and uncertainties.

The concept of immediate transaction finality has profound implications for both financial institutions and their clients. It eliminates the need to wait for days or weeks for a transaction to clear, providing a level of predictability and transparency that is foundational to fostering trust in the cross-border payment process.

Minimizing Counterparty Risks:

The immediacy of real-time settlement significantly mitigates counterparty risks associated with cross-border transactions. In traditional correspondent banking relationships, the extended settlement times expose financial institutions to the risk of default or changes in market conditions. Real-time settlement on RippleNet substantially reduces this risk by minimizing the time during which counterparties are exposed to potential fluctuations in currency values.

The elimination of counterparty risks is particularly crucial in a global financial landscape where volatility is inherent. Financial institutions engaging in cross-border transactions through RippleNet can transact with confidence, knowing that the settlement occurs swiftly, reducing the window for unforeseen events to impact the transaction.

Unlocking Capital and Liquidity:

The real-time settlement feature of RippleNet has a cascading effect on capital and liquidity management for financial institutions. In traditional systems, pre-funding accounts in destination countries is a common practice to ensure timely settlements. This ties up significant amounts of capital that could otherwise be deployed for more strategic purposes.

With real-time settlement, RippleNet obviates the need for pre-funding. Financial institutions can leverage the on-demand liquidity provided by the network, settling transactions in real-time without the need for large capital reserves. This dynamic approach to liquidity management represents a fundamental shift in the way financial institutions allocate and utilize capital, unlocking resources for more productive endeavors.

Enhanced Speed for Cross-Border Transactions:

Speed is a defining characteristic of real-time settlement within RippleNet. The traditional cross-border payment landscape has struggled to keep pace with the immediacy expected in the digital era. Real-time settlement addresses this challenge by reducing transaction times from days to seconds.

Financial institutions leveraging RippleNet can provide their clients with a markedly improved experience. Whether facilitating international trade, supporting remittances, or conducting business transactions, the speed of real-time settlement enhances the overall efficiency and responsiveness of cross-border payments.

Cost Reduction and Operational Efficiency:

The speed and efficiency introduced by real-time settlement directly contribute to cost reduction for financial institutions. In traditional systems, extended settlement times necessitate complex operational processes, involving multiple intermediaries and manual interventions. These processes drive up operational costs and often result in additional fees being passed on to end-users.

RippleNet's real-time settlement, coupled with the elimination of the need for pre-funding, streamlines operational processes. Financial institutions can achieve cost efficiencies by reducing the overhead associated with transaction processing, reconciliation, and liquidity management. This cost-effectiveness positions RippleNet as a compelling solution for financial institutions seeking to enhance their operational efficiency and competitive positioning in the global market.

Customer-Centric Benefits:

Real-time settlement within RippleNet translates into tangible benefits for end-users, whether they are businesses engaged in international trade, individuals sending remittances, or financial entities conducting cross-border transactions. The immediate finality of transactions provides businesses with a more predictable cash flow, reducing the uncertainties associated with delayed settlements.

For individuals relying on remittances, real-time settlement holds the promise of faster, more affordable transactions. The traditional remittance process often involves multiple intermediaries, each adding to the overall cost and time required for funds to reach their destination. RippleNet's real-time settlement minimizes these hurdles, offering a more cost-effective and expeditious solution for individuals globally.

Case Studies Illustrating Real-Time Settlement:

To underscore the practical impact of real-time settlement within RippleNet, it is instructive to examine case studies of financial institutions that have embraced this transformative feature. Santander, a prominent global bank, implemented RippleNet to provide its retail customers with real-time settlement for cross-border transactions. The immediate finality of transactions contributed to a seamless and efficient experience for Santander's customers, setting a precedent for the transformative potential of real-time settlement.

Another notable example is SBI Holdings, a financial conglomerate based in Japan. By leveraging RippleNet's real-time settlement capabilities, SBI Holdings enhanced its remittance services, offering customers faster and more cost-effective cross-border transactions. The speed and efficiency of real-time settlement were pivotal in addressing the evolving needs of SBI Holdings' customer base.

These case studies exemplify how real-time settlement within RippleNet transcends theoretical benefits, translating into tangible improvements in the speed, efficiency, and overall user experience of cross-border payments.

Challenges and Considerations:

While real-time settlement within RippleNet introduces transformative advantages, it is essential to acknowledge the challenges and considerations associated with this paradigm shift. One significant challenge lies in adapting to the real-time nature of transactions. Financial institutions accustomed to the delayed settlement times of traditional systems may need to recalibrate their operational processes and risk management strategies to align with the immediacy of real-time settlement.

The volatility of digital assets, including XRP, which is often used for liquidity in real-time settlement on RippleNet, introduces considerations related to market fluctuations. Financial institutions must navigate the dynamics of digital asset markets and implement risk mitigation strategies to address potential price volatility during the settlement process.

Interoperability with existing financial systems is another consideration. As financial institutions transition to real-time settlement on RippleNet, ensuring compatibility with legacy systems and addressing potential challenges related to integration is crucial. Education and communication efforts are essential to facilitate a smooth transition and build confidence among stakeholders.

In conclusion, real-time settlement within RippleNet represents a watershed moment in the evolution of cross-border payments. The speed, efficiency, and immediate finality introduced by this feature have far-reaching implications for financial institutions, businesses, and individuals engaged in global transactions. As we proceed through subsequent chapters, we will explore additional facets of RippleNet, including the diverse use cases that further contribute to the network's transformative impact on cross-border payments.

Use Cases Across Verticals

The transformative power of RippleNet extends far beyond the realm of traditional cross-border payments. As a decentralized network connecting financial institutions globally, RippleNet opens the door to a diverse array of use cases across various verticals. This chapter explores how RippleNet's versatility and innovative solutions enable a broad spectrum of applications, revolutionizing the way value is transferred and managed across different sectors.

Introduction to Use Cases Across Verticals:

RippleNet's architecture, featuring solutions such as xCurrent, xRapid, and xVia, is not confined to a singular application. Its flexibility allows financial institutions to address a multitude of challenges and capitalize on opportunities across various verticals. By examining specific use cases, we gain insights into how RippleNet transcends traditional boundaries, offering solutions that cater to the unique needs of different industries.

Streamlining Global Trade with RippleNet:

One of the primary use cases of RippleNet extends to the domain of global trade. The inefficiencies in traditional cross-border payments have long hindered the seamless flow of capital between international trading partners. RippleNet addresses this challenge by providing a platform for swift, secure, and cost-effective transactions.

Financial institutions involved in global trade leverage RippleNet to facilitate real-time settlement, reducing the time and friction associated with cross-border transactions. This efficiency is particularly crucial in trade finance, where rapid settlement and transparency in payment flows are essential for businesses engaged in import and export activities.

By streamlining global trade finance, RippleNet contributes to the growth of international commerce. Businesses can optimize their working capital, reduce the risks associated with currency fluctuations, and enhance the overall efficiency of cross-border transactions. This use case is a testament to how RippleNet serves as a catalyst for economic growth and prosperity in the global trade landscape.

Revolutionizing Remittances with xRapid:

Remittances, the lifeblood for many families in emerging markets, have traditionally been marred by high costs and prolonged settlement times. RippleNet's xRapid solution emerges as a game-changer in this vertical, offering on-demand liquidity powered by the digital asset XRP.

Financial institutions leveraging xRapid can source liquidity in real-time through XRP, eliminating the need for pre-funding in destination currencies. This not only reduces costs associated with maintaining pre-funded accounts but also accelerates the speed of remittance transactions.

The use case of xRapid in remittances is exemplified by MoneyGram, a global money transfer company. By integrating xRapid into its operations, MoneyGram achieved significant cost savings and efficiency gains. The immediacy of on-demand liquidity ensures that funds reach their destination swiftly, providing a tangible benefit to individuals relying on remittances for their financial well-being.

Enabling Real-Time Payments in Retail Banking:

Retail banking is another vertical where RippleNet's capabilities are harnessed to enhance the customer experience and streamline payment processes. Santander, one of the world's largest retail banks, implemented RippleNet to offer its retail customers real-time settlement for cross-border transactions.

The use case in retail banking illustrates how RippleNet's immediate transaction finality and efficiency contribute to a seamless banking experience for customers. Retail clients benefit from faster, more transparent international transactions, setting a new standard for the level of service expected in the digital age.

Real-time payments in retail banking are not limited to international transactions. RippleNet's capabilities can also be applied domestically, transforming the landscape of peer-to-peer payments and everyday transactions. The speed and cost-effectiveness introduced by RippleNet align with the evolving expectations of retail banking customers who seek instant and frictionless payment experiences.

Optimizing Corporate Payments with xVia:

Corporate payments, often characterized by complex and cumbersome processes, stand to benefit from RippleNet's xVia solution. xVia serves as a standardized API for payment initiation, allowing businesses to connect with financial institutions globally through a single interface.

This use case addresses the challenges associated with the diversity of payment systems and formats across different regions. xVia simplifies the process of initiating payments, reducing the need for manual interventions and minimizing the risk of errors. Corporate treasurers and finance departments can streamline their payment workflows, achieving greater efficiency and accuracy in cross-border transactions.

MercuryFX, a global currency exchange provider, exemplifies the application of xVia in optimizing corporate payments. By leveraging RippleNet, MercuryFX facilitated cross-border payments in minutes, demonstrating how the network's capabilities extend beyond traditional banking to meet the specific needs of corporate clients.

Opening New Markets with XRP in Financial Services:

Financial services, including remittance providers, currency exchange firms, and other non-banking entities, find new opportunities for growth and market expansion through RippleNet. Cuallix, a financial institution focused on cross-border payments, leveraged XRP to open new markets and enhance its service offerings.

By incorporating XRP into its operations, Cuallix achieved faster and more cost-effective cross-border transactions. The immediate settlement and liquidity benefits of XRP empowered Cuallix to explore new corridors and extend its reach to previously underserved regions.

This use case illustrates how RippleNet's innovative solutions, particularly those leveraging XRP, provide non-traditional financial service providers with the tools to compete on a global scale. The democratization of access to efficient cross-border payment solutions fosters competition and innovation, ultimately benefiting consumers and businesses alike.

Facilitating Real-Time Settlement in E-commerce:

The e-commerce industry, characterized by rapid transactions and global customer bases, demands payment solutions that align with the pace of digital commerce. RippleNet's real-time settlement capabilities position it as an ideal solution for e-commerce platforms seeking to enhance the efficiency of cross-border payments.

E-commerce businesses can leverage RippleNet to provide their customers with real-time settlement, reducing the delays and uncertainties associated with traditional payment methods. The immediacy of settlement aligns with the expectations of modern consumers who prioritize convenience and speed in their online transactions.

The use case in e-commerce is not confined to payment efficiency alone. RippleNet's ability to facilitate micropayments, enabled by the low transaction costs of XRP, opens new possibilities for business models centered around digital content, subscriptions, and other online services. This adaptability to the evolving landscape of digital commerce positions RippleNet as a strategic partner for e-commerce platforms navigating the complexities of cross-border payments.

Driving Financial Inclusion through Mobile Money:

Mobile money services, prevalent in many emerging markets, play a pivotal role in driving financial inclusion. RippleNet's capabilities offer a transformative solution for mobile money providers seeking to enhance the efficiency and accessibility of their services.

By integrating with RippleNet, mobile money operators can tap into the network's real-time settlement and cost-effectiveness. This allows them to offer more competitive international remittance services, facilitating cross-border transactions for individuals who may not have access to traditional banking services.

The use case in mobile money highlights how RippleNet contributes to financial inclusion by empowering mobile money providers to extend their reach globally. This aligns with Ripple's vision of creating an inclusive financial ecosystem where individuals, irrespective of their geographic location, can participate in the global economy.

Smart Contracts and NFTs in the Entertainment Industry:

RippleNet's capabilities extend beyond traditional finance to explore innovative use cases in the entertainment industry. The introduction of smart contracts on RippleNet opens new possibilities for content creators, artists, and entertainment platforms.

Smart contracts facilitate programmable and automated agreements between parties. In the context of the entertainment industry, this could involve royalty payments, licensing agreements, and content distribution contracts. By leveraging smart contracts on RippleNet, participants in the entertainment ecosystem can automate and streamline these complex processes, reducing administrative overhead and ensuring fair and transparent compensation for creators.

The advent of Non-Fungible Tokens (NFTs), representing unique digital assets on a blockchain, further enhances the use cases within the entertainment industry. RippleNet's ability to represent any asset on its ledger provides a foundation for creating, trading, and redeeming tokenized assets, including NFTs. This opens new revenue streams for artists and creators, as well as novel ways for fans to engage with and support their favorite content.

Programmable Finance and Decentralized Finance (DeFi):

RippleNet's foray into programmable finance and decentralized finance (DeFi) reflects a broader shift in the financial industry toward more open, transparent, and programmable systems. RippleNet's smart contract capabilities enable the creation of programmable financial instruments, including swaps, loans, and escrows.

These programmable financial instruments lay the groundwork for decentralized financial services, allowing individuals and businesses to engage in peer-to-peer lending, decentralized exchanges, and other financial activities without the need for traditional intermediaries. RippleNet's architecture, built on the principles of decentralization and interoperability, aligns with the ethos of the broader DeFi movement.

The use case of programmable finance and DeFi on RippleNet signifies the network's commitment to staying at the forefront of financial innovation. As blockchain technology continues to evolve, RippleNet provides a robust foundation for exploring and implementing decentralized financial solutions that empower users and promote financial inclusivity.

Conclusion: The Versatility of RippleNet's Use Cases Across Verticals:

The myriad use cases explored in this chapter underscore the versatility and transformative potential of RippleNet across various verticals. From streamlining global trade to revolutionizing remittances, optimizing corporate payments, enabling real-time transactions in retail banking, and driving financial inclusion through mobile money, RippleNet's impact is felt across the entire spectrum of financial services.

The network's ability to adapt to diverse industries and use cases is a testament to its foundational principles of decentralization, interoperability, and efficiency. As RippleNet continues to evolve, it is poised to shape the future of cross-border payments and redefine the ways in which value is transferred and managed on a global scale. The subsequent chapters will delve deeper into specific components of RippleNet, exploring the role of xCurrent, xRapid, and xVia in delivering these innovative solutions across different verticals.

Chapter 2: xRapid - Leveraging XRP for Liquidity
On-Demand Liquidity Between Currencies

In the ever-evolving landscape of cross-border payments, the concept of liquidity is central to ensuring the smooth and efficient transfer of value between currencies. xRapid, a key component of RippleNet, introduces a groundbreaking solution to the liquidity challenge by leveraging the digital asset XRP. This chapter delves into the intricacies of on-demand liquidity between currencies facilitated by xRapid, exploring how it transforms the traditional dynamics of cross-border transactions.

Introduction to xRapid and Liquidity:

xRapid, as part of Ripple's suite of solutions, addresses a fundamental challenge in cross-border payments — the need for efficient liquidity management. Traditional methods often involve pre-funding accounts in destination currencies, tying up significant capital and introducing complexities in the settlement process. xRapid revolutionizes this paradigm by enabling on-demand liquidity, a dynamic approach that streamlines the movement of value between currencies without the need for large pre-funded reserves.

At the core of xRapid's innovation is the use of XRP, a digital asset native to the Ripple ecosystem. XRP serves as a bridge currency, providing a source of liquidity that transcends traditional banking constraints. This chapter explores how xRapid harnesses the unique properties of XRP to facilitate on-demand liquidity, unlocking new possibilities for financial institutions engaged in cross-border transactions.

The Traditional Liquidity Challenge:

Traditional cross-border payments are often encumbered by the challenge of managing liquidity across different currencies. Financial institutions engaged in international transactions face the dilemma of maintaining pre-funded accounts in multiple currencies to facilitate timely settlements. This practice, while addressing the need for liquidity, comes with significant drawbacks.

Firstly, pre-funding ties up capital that could otherwise be deployed for more strategic purposes. Financial institutions are compelled to allocate substantial resources to maintain liquidity buffers in various currencies, limiting their flexibility and efficiency. Secondly, the reliance on pre-funding introduces operational complexities, requiring meticulous forecasting and management of funds across diverse accounts.

xRapid emerges as a solution to these challenges by introducing a model of on-demand liquidity. Rather than pre-funding accounts, financial institutions can leverage XRP to source liquidity in real-time, precisely when needed for settlement. This dynamic approach not only optimizes capital allocation but also streamlines operational processes, offering a more efficient and cost-effective solution for cross-border payments.

The Role of XRP in On-Demand Liquidity:

Central to xRapid's ability to provide on-demand liquidity is the digital asset XRP. Unlike traditional fiat currencies, XRP operates on a decentralized blockchain, and its unique properties make it an ideal bridge currency for facilitating cross-border transactions.

Liquidity Bridging with XRP: XRP serves as a bridge between two fiat currencies, allowing financial institutions to source liquidity efficiently. When a payment needs to be made from one currency to another, xRapid converts the originating currency into XRP, transfers the XRP across borders, and then converts it back into the destination currency. This process occurs in a matter of seconds, ensuring rapid settlement and minimizing exposure to currency volatility.

The liquidity bridging mechanism with XRP is a departure from traditional correspondent banking models. In the traditional approach, banks maintain nostro and vostro accounts in each other's institutions, pre-funding these accounts to facilitate cross-border transactions. xRapid eliminates the need for these pre-funded accounts by utilizing XRP as a liquidity bridge, making the entire process more streamlined and capital-efficient.

Market-Driven Exchange Rates: The market-driven exchange rates of XRP play a crucial role in ensuring the efficiency of on-demand liquidity. As a digital asset traded on various cryptocurrency exchanges, the value of XRP is determined by market forces. xRapid taps into this market liquidity, providing financial institutions with exchange rates that reflect real-time market conditions.

The use of market-driven exchange rates introduces transparency and fairness into the cross-border payment process. Financial institutions can execute transactions at rates that accurately reflect the current market value of XRP, minimizing the impact of slippage and ensuring that customers receive competitive rates for their international transfers.

Reducing Counterparty Risks: On-demand liquidity with XRP significantly reduces counterparty risks associated with cross-border transactions. In traditional correspondent banking, the settlement process involves multiple intermediaries, each introducing an element of risk. With xRapid, the conversion of one currency to XRP and back to another occurs seamlessly, reducing the number of intermediaries involved and minimizing the potential for errors or delays.

The immediate settlement facilitated by XRP also contributes to risk mitigation. Once a payment is converted into XRP, the transfer and conversion processes occur rapidly, reducing the exposure to fluctuations in currency values. This swift settlement cycle enhances the overall reliability and security of cross-border transactions, addressing a key concern for financial institutions and their clients.

Enhancing Liquidity Pools: xRapid's use of XRP enhances liquidity pools in a way that is not possible with traditional fiat currencies. The global nature of XRP trading across various cryptocurrency exchanges ensures a deep and diverse pool of liquidity. This depth and diversity contribute to the resilience and stability of on-demand liquidity, even during periods of high transaction volume.

Financial institutions leveraging xRapid can tap into this expansive liquidity pool, accessing the liquidity they need precisely when required. The efficiency of XRP as a bridge currency, coupled with its widespread availability on cryptocurrency exchanges, ensures that on-demand liquidity remains a reliable and scalable solution for cross-border payments.

Case Studies Illustrating On-Demand Liquidity with xRapid:

Examining real-world case studies provides concrete examples of how on-demand liquidity with xRapid transforms cross-border payments. MoneyGram, a global money transfer company, stands as a prominent example of a financial institution that embraced xRapid to enhance liquidity management and improve the efficiency of its remittance services.

MoneyGram's Journey with xRapid: MoneyGram's partnership with Ripple and adoption of xRapid marked a significant shift in the company's approach to cross-border payments. By leveraging XRP as a bridge currency, MoneyGram achieved substantial cost savings and efficiency gains in its remittance services. The immediacy of on-demand liquidity enabled MoneyGram to settle transactions in a matter of seconds, providing a stark contrast to the delays associated with traditional settlement processes.

The success of MoneyGram's implementation of xRapid underscores the tangible benefits of on-demand liquidity in a real-world financial environment. As a result of this success, other financial institutions and remittance providers have increasingly explored the adoption of xRapid, signaling a broader industry acknowledgment of the transformative potential of on-demand liquidity.

Challenges and Considerations:

While on-demand liquidity with xRapid introduces groundbreaking advantages, it is essential to acknowledge the challenges and considerations associated with this innovative approach.

Regulatory Landscape: Navigating the regulatory landscape remains a significant consideration for financial institutions leveraging on-demand liquidity with xRapid. The regulatory environment for digital assets, including XRP, varies across jurisdictions, and financial institutions must ensure compliance with applicable regulations. Ripple's proactive engagement with regulators and commitment to compliance aims to address these concerns, fostering a regulatory environment conducive to the broader adoption of on-demand liquidity.

Market Volatility: The volatility inherent in cryptocurrency markets, including the market for XRP, introduces considerations related to price fluctuations. While on-demand liquidity is designed to mitigate exposure to currency volatility during the swift settlement process, financial institutions must implement risk management strategies to address potential price fluctuations. Initiatives such as Ripple's Market Insights seek to provide real-time data and analysis to support informed decision-making in the face of market volatility.

Education and Adoption: The transition to on-demand liquidity with xRapid requires education and adoption efforts within the financial industry. Financial institutions, including banks and payment service providers, may need to familiarize themselves with the mechanics of on-demand liquidity and assess its compatibility with their existing systems and processes.

Ripple's engagement with its network of partners, combined with educational initiatives, aims to facilitate a smooth transition and foster confidence in the transformative potential of on-demand liquidity.

Conclusion: The Paradigm Shift of On-Demand Liquidity:

On-demand liquidity with xRapid represents a paradigm shift in the realm of cross-border payments. By leveraging the digital asset XRP as a bridge currency, xRapid introduces a dynamic model that challenges the traditional notions of liquidity management. Financial institutions, remittance providers, and other stakeholders in the cross-border payment ecosystem are presented with an innovative solution that optimizes capital allocation, reduces operational complexities, and enhances the overall efficiency of international transactions.

As we progress through subsequent chapters, we will further explore the impact of xRapid on cross-border payments, examining its role in unlocking new corridors, fostering financial inclusion, and contributing to the broader evolution of RippleNet's ecosystem. On-demand liquidity with xRapid exemplifies the transformative potential of blockchain and digital assets in reshaping the future of finance and value transfer on a global scale.

Faster Access to Emerging Market Corridors

In the dynamic landscape of cross-border payments, emerging markets often pose unique challenges due to factors such as limited banking infrastructure, currency volatility, and regulatory complexities. xRapid, a pivotal component of Ripple's suite of solutions, emerges as a transformative force in this context, providing faster access to emerging market corridors. This chapter explores how xRapid, by leveraging the digital asset XRP, addresses the specific challenges associated with emerging markets, unlocking new possibilities for financial institutions and fostering inclusive economic growth.

Introduction to Emerging Market Corridors:

Emerging markets play a crucial role in the global economy, representing regions with expanding economic potential, diverse consumer bases, and untapped opportunities. However, the traditional cross-border payment landscape has often struggled to provide efficient and accessible solutions for transactions involving emerging market currencies. Challenges such as limited banking infrastructure, currency illiquidity, and regulatory complexities create barriers that impede the seamless flow of value.

xRapid steps into this arena as a solution designed to bridge these gaps and facilitate faster access to emerging market corridors. By leveraging the speed and efficiency of XRP, xRapid transforms the traditional narrative surrounding cross-border payments in emerging markets, enabling financial institutions to navigate these challenges with agility and confidence.

The Challenges of Emerging Market Corridors:

Emerging markets present a unique set of challenges that can hinder the efficiency of cross-border payments. Understanding these challenges is essential to appreciating the transformative impact that xRapid can have in addressing them.

Limited Banking Infrastructure: Many emerging markets lack a robust banking infrastructure, with a significant portion of the population remaining unbanked or underbanked. This scarcity of traditional banking services complicates the process of initiating and receiving cross-border payments, particularly in regions where financial institutions are scarce or inaccessible.

Currency Volatility: Emerging market currencies often exhibit higher levels of volatility compared to major fiat currencies. This volatility introduces uncertainty and risk into cross-border transactions, as fluctuations in currency values can impact the final settlement amount. Managing this volatility is a crucial consideration for financial institutions engaging in transactions with emerging market currencies.

Regulatory Complexities: Navigating diverse and evolving regulatory landscapes is a common challenge in emerging markets. Regulatory frameworks governing cross-border payments can vary widely, and financial institutions must adapt to the regulatory requirements of each jurisdiction in which they operate. This complexity adds an additional layer of friction to the cross-border payment process.

How xRapid Addresses Challenges in Emerging Markets:

xRapid, powered by the digital asset XRP, introduces a set of features and capabilities specifically designed to address the challenges associated with emerging market corridors. By leveraging the unique properties of XRP, xRapid offers financial institutions a solution that enhances speed, reduces costs, and navigates the intricacies of emerging market dynamics.

Swift and Cost-Effective Transactions: One of the primary advantages of xRapid in emerging markets is its ability to facilitate swift and cost-effective transactions. The use of XRP as a bridge currency streamlines the conversion process between different fiat currencies, reducing the time required for settlement. This speed is particularly impactful in regions where traditional banking infrastructure is limited, providing a more efficient alternative for cross-border transactions.

The cost-effectiveness of xRapid in emerging markets is a result of its on-demand liquidity model. Financial institutions no longer need to maintain large pre-funded accounts in various currencies, reducing the associated costs. xRapid's reliance on XRP as a liquidity bridge enables financial institutions to optimize capital allocation and offer more competitive rates for cross-border transactions involving emerging market currencies.

Mitigating Currency Volatility: Currency volatility, a common challenge in emerging markets, is mitigated through xRapid's swift settlement process. By converting originating currency into XRP, transferring XRP across borders, and converting it back into the destination currency in a matter of seconds, xRapid minimizes the exposure to currency fluctuations. This immediate settlement cycle reduces the window during which the transaction is susceptible to volatility, providing a level of predictability and risk mitigation for financial institutions operating in emerging markets.

The use of XRP as a bridge currency also contributes to stability in the settlement process. XRP's market-driven exchange rates, reflecting real-time market conditions, offer financial institutions transparency and accuracy in determining the value of transactions. This transparency is particularly beneficial in emerging markets where currency values can experience rapid and unpredictable changes.

Overcoming Limited Banking Infrastructure: Limited banking infrastructure in emerging markets often impedes the accessibility of traditional cross-border payment services. xRapid, by leveraging the decentralized nature of blockchain and XRP, transcends the constraints of traditional banking systems. Financial institutions using xRapid can extend their reach to regions with limited banking infrastructure, providing individuals and businesses with access to efficient and inclusive cross-border payment solutions.

The accessibility offered by xRapid aligns with Ripple's vision of creating a more inclusive financial ecosystem. In regions where traditional banking services are scarce, xRapid empowers financial institutions to reach underserved populations, fostering financial inclusion and contributing to the broader goal of reducing global economic disparities.

Navigating Regulatory Complexities: Regulatory complexities often present hurdles in emerging markets, requiring financial institutions to navigate a complex web of rules and compliance requirements. xRapid, as part of Ripple's commitment to regulatory compliance, is designed to facilitate adherence to regulatory frameworks.

Ripple actively engages with regulators worldwide, seeking to create an environment that encourages the responsible adoption of blockchain and digital assets. This proactive engagement not only supports the broader acceptance of xRapid but also contributes to the establishment of clear regulatory guidelines that facilitate the integration of emerging markets into the global financial system.

Case Studies Illustrating Faster Access to Emerging Market Corridors with xRapid:

Examining real-world case studies provides tangible examples of how xRapid's on-demand liquidity model accelerates access to emerging market corridors, demonstrating its impact on financial institutions and the individuals and businesses they serve.

Enhancing Financial Inclusion with SendFriend: SendFriend, a FinTech company focused on providing remittance services, serves as a compelling example of how xRapid fosters financial inclusion in emerging markets. By leveraging xRapid and XRP, SendFriend reduced the cost of remittance transactions and accelerated settlement times for customers sending money to the Philippines.

The use of xRapid allowed SendFriend to offer more competitive rates for cross-border transactions, providing a tangible benefit to individuals in the Philippines who rely on remittances for their financial well-being. The efficiency and cost-effectiveness introduced by xRapid contribute to a more inclusive remittance ecosystem, illustrating how blockchain technology can bridge gaps and empower individuals in emerging markets.

Opening New Corridors with Viamericas: Viamericas, a leading cross-border payments provider, exemplifies how xRapid opens new corridors and enhances access to emerging markets. By integrating xRapid into its operations, Viamericas expanded its remittance services to Mexico, providing faster and more cost-effective transactions for customers in both the United States and Mexico.

The ability of xRapid to open new corridors aligns with its broader impact on fostering global financial connectivity. Financial institutions, enabled by xRapid, can explore and enter markets that were previously challenging to access due to limited banking infrastructure and regulatory complexities. This expansion of corridors contributes to the growth of cross-border payments and promotes economic interconnectedness between regions.

Challenges and Considerations in Emerging Markets:

While xRapid addresses many challenges associated with emerging market corridors, it is essential to acknowledge the nuanced landscape and consider potential challenges and considerations specific to these regions.

Educational Initiatives: Educational initiatives play a crucial role in fostering the adoption of xRapid in emerging markets. Financial institutions, businesses, and individuals may require comprehensive understanding and training to fully leverage the benefits of xRapid. Ripple's commitment to educational initiatives aims to bridge this knowledge gap, empowering stakeholders in emerging markets to embrace the advantages of blockchain and digital assets.

Infrastructure Development: The success of xRapid in emerging markets is closely tied to the development of necessary infrastructure. This includes not only technological infrastructure to support blockchain-based solutions but also improvements in connectivity, access to the internet, and the overall digital readiness of the population. Collaborative efforts between financial institutions, technology providers, and governments can contribute to the development of a robust ecosystem that facilitates the seamless integration of xRapid.

Regulatory Harmonization: The regulatory landscape in emerging markets can be complex and fragmented. Harmonizing regulatory frameworks across different jurisdictions is a consideration for the sustainable growth of xRapid in these regions. Ripple's ongoing engagement with regulators globally aims to contribute to regulatory harmonization, creating an environment that fosters innovation while ensuring compliance with local laws.

Conclusion: Accelerating Financial Connectivity in Emerging Markets:

Faster access to emerging market corridors is a key dimension of xRapid's impact on the cross-border payments landscape. By addressing the challenges of limited banking infrastructure, currency volatility, and regulatory complexities, xRapid, powered by XRP, accelerates the pace of financial connectivity between regions. Financial institutions leveraging xRapid gain a competitive edge in providing efficient and inclusive cross-border payment services, contributing to the growth of emerging markets and the global economy.

As we progress through subsequent chapters, we will continue to explore the multifaceted role of xRapid, examining its influence on diverse aspects of cross-border payments. From unlocking new corridors to minimizing counterparty risks and enhancing financial inclusion, xRapid's impact on emerging markets is a testament to the transformative potential of blockchain technology and digital assets in reshaping the future of finance on a global scale.

XRP Minimized Costs and Unlocked Capital

In the intricate realm of cross-border payments, cost efficiency and capital optimization stand as paramount considerations for financial institutions. xRapid, a pivotal component of Ripple's suite of solutions, emerges as a transformative force in this regard, minimizing costs and unlocking capital through its innovative use of the digital asset XRP. This chapter delves into the intricacies of how xRapid reshapes the cost dynamics of cross-border transactions, offering financial institutions a more capital-efficient alternative and fostering a new era of financial flexibility.

Introduction to Cost Dynamics in Cross-Border Payments:

The traditional landscape of cross-border payments has long been characterized by intricate cost structures, often marked by inefficiencies, hidden fees, and a reliance on pre-funded accounts. Financial institutions navigating these complexities face challenges related to capital allocation, operational costs, and the need to maintain liquidity buffers in various currencies. xRapid, with its emphasis on on-demand liquidity and the utilization of XRP, introduces a paradigm shift in cost dynamics, minimizing expenses and unlocking capital for more strategic purposes.

Challenges in Traditional Cost Structures:

Understanding the challenges embedded in traditional cost structures is essential to appreciating the groundbreaking impact of xRapid in reshaping the financial landscape.

Pre-Funding and Capital Tie-Up: Traditional cross-border payments often involve the pre-funding of accounts in destination currencies. This practice ties up significant amounts of capital that could otherwise be deployed for more strategic purposes. Financial institutions must maintain reserves in multiple currencies, leading to capital inefficiencies and limitations on their ability to allocate resources dynamically.

Opaque Fee Structures: The fee structures associated with traditional cross-border payments can be opaque and convoluted. Intermediaries along the payment chain introduce additional costs, and customers may incur fees that are not transparently communicated. This lack of transparency impacts the overall cost-effectiveness of cross-border transactions and diminishes the value proposition for both financial institutions and end-users.

Operational Inefficiencies: Traditional correspondent banking models can introduce operational inefficiencies, including delays in settlement, manual reconciliation processes, and an increased risk of errors. These inefficiencies not only contribute to higher operational costs but also hinder the ability of financial institutions to provide seamless and timely cross-border payment services.

How xRapid Minimizes Costs:

xRapid, through its innovative use of XRP, introduces a set of features and mechanisms that specifically target the cost challenges prevalent in traditional cross-border payments.

On-Demand Liquidity Model: At the core of xRapid's cost-minimization strategy is its on-demand liquidity model. Instead of pre-funding accounts in various currencies, financial institutions leveraging xRapid source liquidity in real-time through XRP. This dynamic approach eliminates the need for large capital reserves and introduces a level of flexibility that is not achievable with traditional pre-funding methods.

The on-demand liquidity model ensures that financial institutions allocate capital precisely when needed for settlement. This minimizes the capital tie-up associated with maintaining pre-funded accounts, allowing financial institutions to optimize their capital allocation and direct resources to areas that yield higher returns or strategic value.

XRP as a Bridge Currency: XRP, as the digital asset native to the Ripple ecosystem, plays a pivotal role in minimizing costs within the xRapid framework. Acting as a bridge currency, XRP enables the seamless conversion of one fiat currency into another, reducing the need for multiple intermediaries and the associated fees.

The use of XRP as a bridge currency enhances cost efficiency by streamlining the settlement process. Financial institutions leveraging xRapid can achieve immediate settlement by converting originating currency into XRP, transferring XRP across borders, and converting it back into the destination currency in a matter of seconds. This rapid settlement cycle reduces the time during which capital is tied up and minimizes the exposure to currency volatility, contributing to overall cost savings.

Market-Driven Exchange Rates: xRapid's utilization of market-driven exchange rates further enhances cost efficiency in cross-border payments. XRP's value is determined by market forces on various cryptocurrency exchanges, reflecting real-time market conditions. Financial institutions executing transactions through xRapid benefit from exchange rates that are transparent, competitive, and reflective of the current market value of XRP.

The market-driven exchange rates introduce transparency into the cost structure of cross-border transactions, allowing financial institutions to provide more accurate and competitive rates to their customers. This transparency aligns with Ripple's commitment to fostering fair and efficient financial ecosystems.

Reduced Intermediary Costs: Traditional correspondent banking models often involve multiple intermediaries along the payment chain, each introducing additional costs. xRapid's streamlined process, facilitated by XRP as a bridge currency, reduces the number of intermediaries involved in cross-border transactions. This reduction in intermediaries not only accelerates settlement times but also contributes to overall cost savings.

The immediate settlement facilitated by xRapid with XRP as a bridge currency eliminates the need for extensive correspondent banking relationships, further reducing the costs associated with intermediaries. Financial institutions leveraging xRapid can offer more competitive rates to their customers while maintaining or improving their profit margins.

Unlocking Capital for Strategic Deployment:

Beyond minimizing costs, xRapid's impact extends to unlocking capital for financial institutions, providing newfound flexibility for strategic deployment.

Optimized Capital Allocation: The on-demand liquidity model employed by xRapid enables financial institutions to optimize their capital allocation. Instead of holding significant reserves in various currencies, which would otherwise be idle or generate minimal returns, financial institutions can dynamically allocate capital precisely when and where it is needed for settlement.

This optimized capital allocation aligns with broader strategic goals, allowing financial institutions to deploy resources in a manner that maximizes returns and supports initiatives such as innovation, expansion into new markets, or investment in technology.

Enhanced Liquidity Management: Traditional correspondent banking models often require financial institutions to maintain liquidity buffers in anticipation of potential payment flows. xRapid's real-time liquidity sourcing through XRP enhances liquidity management by providing financial institutions with the ability to access liquidity precisely when required for settlement.

The enhanced liquidity management facilitated by xRapid allows financial institutions to operate with leaner capital reserves, reducing the need for excess liquidity buffers. This not only contributes to cost savings but also unlocks capital that can be redirected toward growth-oriented initiatives or used to enhance overall financial resilience.

Strategic Investments and Partnerships: With minimized costs and unlocked capital, financial institutions leveraging xRapid are better positioned to make strategic investments and forge partnerships that drive long-term value. The newfound financial flexibility enables institutions to explore opportunities for innovation, collaborate with FinTechs, and invest in technologies that enhance their competitive edge in the rapidly evolving financial landscape.

Strategic investments and partnerships can include initiatives such as upgrading technology infrastructure, exploring blockchain-based solutions beyond cross-border payments, or engaging in collaborative efforts that contribute to the broader evolution of the financial ecosystem.

Case Studies Illustrating Cost Minimization and Capital Unlocking with xRapid:

Examining real-world case studies provides tangible examples of how xRapid's cost-minimization strategies and capital unlocking mechanisms impact financial institutions.

Reducing Remittance Costs with Cuallix: Cuallix, a financial institution focusing on cross-border payments and remittances, implemented xRapid to reduce remittance costs and enhance the efficiency of its payment services. By leveraging xRapid and XRP, Cuallix achieved significant cost savings compared to traditional remittance methods.

The immediate settlement capabilities of xRapid minimized the need for extensive capital tied up in pre-funded accounts, allowing Cuallix to allocate capital more efficiently. The reduction in operational costs and intermediaries contributed to an overall enhancement of Cuallix's cost structure, making cross-border payments more affordable for its customers.

Unlocking Capital for Expansion with MercuryFX: MercuryFX, a global currency specialist, utilized xRapid to unlock capital for strategic expansion into new markets. By adopting xRapid's on-demand liquidity model, MercuryFX reduced the need for extensive pre-funding of accounts and optimized its capital allocation for real-time settlement.

The capital unlocked through xRapid empowered MercuryFX to explore new corridors and expand its footprint in the cross-border payments landscape. This strategic deployment of capital aligned with MercuryFX's growth objectives, showcasing how xRapid's impact extends beyond cost minimization to unlocking resources for business expansion.

Challenges and Considerations in Cost Minimization and Capital Unlocking:

While xRapid introduces groundbreaking advantages in cost minimization and capital unlocking, it is essential to acknowledge potential challenges and considerations associated with its adoption.

Integration Challenges: Integrating xRapid into existing banking infrastructure may pose challenges for some financial institutions. Compatibility with legacy systems, adherence to regulatory requirements, and the need for staff training are factors that institutions must carefully consider to ensure a seamless transition.

Educational Efforts: Ensuring that stakeholders, including financial institution staff and end-users, understand the benefits and mechanics of xRapid is crucial for its successful adoption. Ripple's educational initiatives and collaborative efforts with industry partners aim to address this challenge by providing comprehensive resources and support for institutions venturing into the world of blockchain-based solutions.

Risk Management: While xRapid minimizes certain risks associated with traditional correspondent banking, financial institutions must implement robust risk management strategies to address potential risks related to market volatility, regulatory changes, and technology vulnerabilities. Proactive risk management practices are integral to maintaining the security and stability of cross-border transactions facilitated by xRapid.

Conclusion: Reshaping Cost Dynamics and Financial Flexibility:

xRapid's role in minimizing costs and unlocking capital represents a significant paradigm shift in the landscape of cross-border payments. By leveraging the on-demand liquidity model and the innovative use of XRP as a bridge currency, xRapid introduces efficiencies that redefine the cost structure of cross-border transactions. Financial institutions leveraging xRapid not only achieve cost savings but also unlock capital for strategic initiatives, fostering a new era of financial flexibility and resilience.

As we progress through subsequent chapters, we will further explore the multifaceted impact of xRapid on cross-border payments. From minimizing counterparty risks to fostering financial inclusion, xRapid's influence extends across diverse dimensions, contributing to the broader evolution of RippleNet's ecosystem and reshaping the future of value transfer on a global scale.

Partner Financial Institutions

In the transformative landscape of cross-border payments, the collaborative engagement of financial institutions becomes a cornerstone for success. xRapid, an integral component of Ripple's suite of solutions, not only introduces innovative ways to enhance liquidity and reduce costs but also relies on strategic partnerships with financial institutions around the globe. This chapter delves into the significance of partner financial institutions in the adoption and success of xRapid, exploring how collaboration shapes the future of cross-border payments.

Introduction to Partner Financial Institutions:

The success of xRapid is intricately tied to its ability to forge strategic partnerships with financial institutions globally. These partnerships extend beyond mere adoption; they represent a collaborative effort to reshape the traditional paradigms of cross-border payments, bringing about efficiency, speed, and cost-effectiveness. As we explore the role of partner financial institutions in the xRapid ecosystem, we will delve into the motivations, benefits, and collaborative strategies that underpin these transformative relationships.

The Motivations for Partnering with xRapid:

Understanding the motivations that drive financial institutions to partner with xRapid is fundamental to appreciating the symbiotic relationship between technology providers and traditional financial entities.

Access to Innovative Technology: Partnering with xRapid provides financial institutions with access to cutting-edge blockchain technology and the benefits it brings to cross-border payments. The utilization of distributed ledger technology (DLT) and the innovative use of XRP as a bridge currency distinguish xRapid from traditional correspondent banking models. Financial institutions, by embracing xRapid, position themselves at the forefront of technological innovation in the financial sector.

Access to innovative technology not only enhances the operational capabilities of financial institutions but also aligns with the broader industry trend of adopting digital solutions to meet the evolving needs of customers in an increasingly interconnected world.

Efficiency Gains in Cross-Border Payments: Partnering with xRapid enables financial institutions to realize efficiency gains in cross-border payments. The on-demand liquidity model, facilitated by XRP, minimizes the need for pre-funding accounts in various currencies. This reduction in capital tie-up, coupled with the streamlined settlement process, translates into faster and more cost-effective cross-border transactions.

Efficiency gains resonate not only with financial institutions but also with end-users who experience swifter and more affordable international payments. By offering a solution that addresses the challenges of traditional cross-border payments, financial institutions enhance their competitiveness and contribute to a positive customer experience.

Cost Savings and Capital Optimization: Cost considerations are pivotal for financial institutions seeking to maintain competitiveness and financial resilience. Partnering with xRapid allows financial institutions to minimize costs associated with traditional correspondent banking models. The use of XRP as a bridge currency introduces transparency into the cost structure of cross-border transactions, reduces intermediary costs, and optimizes capital allocation.

The cost savings and capital optimization achieved through xRapid's on-demand liquidity model offer financial institutions a tangible competitive advantage. The ability to provide more cost-effective cross-border payment services positions partner financial institutions as leaders in a landscape where efficiency and affordability are increasingly valued by customers.

Strategic Positioning for Future Growth: Partnerships with xRapid contribute to the strategic positioning of financial institutions for future growth and relevance in the evolving financial ecosystem. As the industry undergoes digital transformation, financial institutions that embrace innovative solutions are better positioned to adapt to changing customer expectations, regulatory environments, and technological advancements.

Strategic positioning extends beyond immediate cost savings and efficiency gains; it encompasses the ability of partner financial institutions to remain agile and responsive to emerging trends. By aligning with xRapid, financial institutions signal their commitment to a future where blockchain technology and digital assets play a central role in the global financial landscape.

Benefits for Partner Financial Institutions:

The collaboration between xRapid and partner financial institutions yields a multitude of benefits that extend beyond the immediate adoption of innovative technology.

Enhanced Liquidity Management: Partner financial institutions benefit from enhanced liquidity management facilitated by xRapid. The on-demand liquidity model allows institutions to source liquidity precisely when needed for settlement, eliminating the need for extensive pre-funding of accounts. This dynamic liquidity management aligns with the broader goals of financial institutions to operate efficiently and optimize the use of capital.

The enhanced liquidity management provided by xRapid not only reduces the need for excess liquidity buffers but also empowers financial institutions to navigate fluctuations in payment flows with greater flexibility. This adaptability is crucial in a global financial landscape where market conditions and customer demands can evolve rapidly.

Global Reach and New Corridor Exploration: Partnering with xRapid expands the global reach of financial institutions, allowing them to explore new corridors and markets. The efficient cross-border payment capabilities provided by xRapid enable institutions to extend their services to regions that may have been challenging to access due to limited banking infrastructure, regulatory complexities, or operational inefficiencies.

The global reach facilitated by xRapid aligns with the broader trend of financial institutions seeking to become more interconnected and inclusive. By exploring new corridors, partner financial institutions contribute to the growth of cross-border payments and foster economic interconnectedness between regions.

Competitive Edge in Customer Experience: Financial institutions that partner with xRapid gain a competitive edge in providing an enhanced customer experience. The efficiency gains and cost savings achieved through xRapid's on-demand liquidity model translate into faster, more affordable, and more transparent cross-border transactions for end-users.

The ability to offer a superior customer experience becomes a distinguishing factor in a competitive financial landscape. Partner financial institutions can leverage their collaboration with xRapid as a key selling point, attracting customers who prioritize efficiency, affordability, and transparency in their international transactions.

Strategic Resource Allocation: Partnering with xRapid enables financial institutions to strategically allocate resources for optimal outcomes. The minimized costs and unlocked capital associated with xRapid's on-demand liquidity model allow institutions to redirect resources toward strategic initiatives, technology upgrades, and innovations that contribute to long-term growth.

Strategic resource allocation aligns with the broader goal of financial institutions to position themselves as agile and forward-thinking entities in a rapidly evolving financial ecosystem. By embracing xRapid, partner financial institutions demonstrate a commitment to leveraging technology for strategic advantage.

Collaborative Strategies between xRapid and Partner Financial Institutions:

The successful integration of xRapid into the operations of partner financial institutions involves collaborative strategies that align with the goals and aspirations of both parties.

Technology Integration and Compatibility: One of the primary collaborative efforts involves the seamless integration of xRapid into the existing technology infrastructure of partner financial institutions. This integration requires compatibility with legacy systems, adherence to regulatory requirements, and comprehensive staff training to ensure a smooth transition.

Ripple, as the provider of xRapid, works closely with partner financial institutions to facilitate the integration process. This collaborative approach aims to minimize disruptions and ensure that xRapid becomes an integral and interoperable component of the institution's cross-border payment capabilities.

Educational Initiatives and Stakeholder Engagement: Educational initiatives play a crucial role in ensuring the successful adoption of xRapid by partner financial institutions. Ripple actively engages in educational efforts to provide comprehensive resources and support for institutions venturing into the world of blockchain-based solutions.

These educational initiatives extend beyond the internal staff of financial institutions to include end-users and stakeholders. Ensuring a comprehensive understanding of xRapid's benefits and mechanics contributes to a smoother adoption process and fosters confidence in the transformative potential of the technology.

Regulatory Compliance and Advocacy: Navigating regulatory landscapes is a shared responsibility between xRapid and partner financial institutions. Ripple actively engages with regulators globally to create an environment that encourages the responsible adoption of blockchain and digital assets. This proactive regulatory advocacy aims to contribute to the establishment of clear guidelines that facilitate the integration of xRapid into the global financial system.

Partner financial institutions, in turn, play a crucial role in ensuring compliance with local regulations. Collaborative efforts in regulatory compliance contribute to the long-term sustainability and acceptance of xRapid within the broader financial ecosystem.

Strategic Planning and Roadmap Alignment: Collaborative strategies extend to strategic planning and aligning roadmaps between xRapid and partner financial institutions. Understanding the goals and aspirations of each institution allows for the development of a roadmap that maximizes the impact of xRapid on the institution's cross-border payment capabilities.

Strategic planning involves considerations such as the exploration of new corridors, the integration of additional services, and the continuous evolution of technology to meet emerging market demands. Aligning roadmaps ensures that xRapid remains a dynamic and responsive solution that adapts to the evolving needs of partner financial institutions.

Case Studies Illustrating Successful Partnerships:

Examining real-world case studies provides tangible examples of how successful partnerships between xRapid and financial institutions contribute to the transformation of cross-border payments.

Enhancing Payment Efficiency with Euro Exim Bank: Euro Exim Bank, a financial institution specializing in trade finance, collaborated with xRapid to enhance the efficiency of its cross-border payments. By leveraging xRapid's on-demand liquidity model and the use of XRP, Euro Exim Bank achieved immediate settlement, reduced costs, and optimized capital allocation.

The partnership with xRapid allowed Euro Exim Bank to streamline its cross-border payment processes, providing customers with faster and more cost-effective international transactions. The success of this collaboration underscores the tangible benefits that financial institutions can realize by embracing innovative solutions.

Facilitating Financial Inclusion with SendFriend: SendFriend, a FinTech company focused on providing remittance services, partnered with xRapid to facilitate financial inclusion and reduce the costs of remittances. By utilizing xRapid and XRP, SendFriend reduced remittance costs and accelerated settlement times for customers sending money to the Philippines.

The collaboration between SendFriend and xRapid highlights the role of technology in fostering financial inclusion. The efficiency gains and cost savings realized through xRapid contribute to a more inclusive remittance ecosystem, providing tangible benefits to individuals who rely on cross-border payments for their financial well-being.

Challenges and Considerations in Collaborative Partnerships:

While the collaborative partnerships between xRapid and financial institutions bring about transformative advantages, certain challenges and considerations merit attention.

Navigating Technology Integration Challenges: Integrating xRapid into existing technology infrastructure may pose challenges for some financial institutions. Compatibility with legacy systems, data security considerations, and the need for comprehensive staff training are factors that institutions must carefully navigate to ensure a seamless transition.

The collaborative approach between xRapid and financial institutions involves active engagement to address technology integration challenges and foster a smooth adoption process.

Overcoming Educational Barriers: Educational initiatives play a vital role in overcoming barriers associated with the adoption of innovative solutions like xRapid. Financial institutions may face challenges in ensuring that their staff and end-users have a comprehensive understanding of the benefits and mechanics of xRapid.

Collaborative efforts in educational initiatives aim to bridge this knowledge gap and foster a shared understanding of the transformative potential of xRapid in reshaping the cross-border payments landscape.

Adapting to Regulatory Changes: Navigating regulatory landscapes poses an ongoing challenge for financial institutions adopting blockchain-based solutions. Regulatory changes can impact the adoption and operation of technologies like xRapid, requiring collaborative efforts between technology providers and financial institutions to ensure compliance.

Proactive engagement with regulators, advocacy for clear regulatory guidelines, and a collaborative approach to adapting to regulatory changes contribute to the long-term success of partnerships between xRapid and financial institutions.

Conclusion: The Collaborative Future of Cross-Border Payments:

The collaborative partnerships between xRapid and financial institutions exemplify the transformative potential of technology in reshaping the future of cross-border payments. As financial institutions embrace xRapid's innovative solutions, they position themselves as leaders in a landscape where efficiency, transparency, and strategic resource allocation are paramount.

As we progress through subsequent chapters, we will further explore the multifaceted impact of xRapid on cross-border payments. From unlocking new corridors to fostering financial inclusion and minimizing counterparty risks, xRapid's collaborative partnerships play a pivotal role in shaping the broader evolution of RippleNet's ecosystem and the future of value transfer on a global scale.

Chapter 3: xCurrent - Interledger for Payment Tracking
Send Payment Info and End-to-End Tracking

In the dynamic landscape of cross-border payments, transparency and traceability stand as pillars of trust and efficiency. xCurrent, a fundamental component of Ripple's suite of solutions, introduces a paradigm shift by leveraging Interledger Protocol (ILP) to enable seamless communication between financial institutions. This chapter delves into the pivotal subtopic of "Send Payment Info and End-to-End Tracking," exploring how xCurrent revolutionizes payment tracking, enhances transparency, and establishes a foundation for the future of cross-border transactions.

Introduction to xCurrent and Interledger Protocol:

Before delving into the intricacies of payment tracking, it's essential to understand the foundational elements of xCurrent and the Interledger Protocol (ILP).

xCurrent: xCurrent serves as Ripple's enterprise solution designed to facilitate real-time, cross-border payments between financial institutions. Unlike traditional correspondent banking systems, xCurrent provides a messaging layer that enables secure and instant communication between parties involved in a payment transaction. Its functionality extends beyond simple messaging, incorporating features that enhance transparency, reduce friction, and expedite settlement.

Interledger Protocol (ILP): At the core of xCurrent's ability to send payment information and enable end-to-end tracking is the Interledger Protocol (ILP). ILP is an open standard protocol suite that facilitates payments across different ledgers and payment networks. It acts as a connector, allowing interoperability between diverse financial systems and enabling the seamless flow of payment information. ILP serves as the backbone for xCurrent, fostering a new era of connectivity in cross-border payments.

The Essence of Sending Payment Information:

Traditional cross-border payments often involve a lack of transparency and delayed communication between financial institutions along the payment chain. xCurrent addresses this challenge by introducing a streamlined process for sending payment information in real-time. This process not only expedites the overall transaction but also enhances the ability of financial institutions to make informed decisions based on up-to-date information.

Real-Time Communication: One of the key features of xCurrent is its ability to enable real-time communication between sending and receiving parties. As a payment progresses through the different stages of the transaction lifecycle, xCurrent ensures that relevant information is transmitted instantly. This real-time communication stands in stark contrast to traditional correspondent banking, where delays and opacity in information flow can lead to inefficiencies and uncertainties.

Comprehensive Payment Details: xCurrent goes beyond the basic transmission of payment initiation messages. It includes a comprehensive set of payment details that accompany the transaction, providing a rich dataset for both the sending and receiving financial institutions. This dataset encompasses information such as the originator, beneficiary, transaction amount, and any relevant compliance or regulatory details.

The inclusion of comprehensive payment details enhances the overall transparency of cross-border transactions. Financial institutions leveraging xCurrent gain access to a wealth of information, allowing for better risk assessment, regulatory compliance, and decision-making throughout the payment lifecycle.

Mitigating Information Asymmetry: In traditional correspondent banking models, information asymmetry often arises due to delays in the transmission of payment information. xCurrent addresses this challenge by mitigating information asymmetry through its real-time communication capabilities. Both the sending and receiving financial institutions have synchronized access to the latest payment information, reducing the likelihood of misunderstandings or discrepancies.

Mitigating information asymmetry contributes to a more collaborative and efficient cross-border payment ecosystem. Financial institutions can operate with a shared understanding of the transaction, fostering trust and reducing the need for manual intervention or reconciliation.

Empowering End-to-End Tracking:

End-to-end tracking is a transformative aspect of xCurrent's capabilities, providing unprecedented visibility into the cross-border payment process. This functionality enhances accountability, reduces settlement risks, and sets the stage for a future where the entire journey of a payment can be traced with precision.

Tracking the Payment Lifecycle: xCurrent allows financial institutions to track the entire lifecycle of a payment in real-time. From the moment the payment is initiated to its final settlement, each stage is recorded and made accessible to all relevant parties. This end-to-end tracking capability represents a departure from the fragmented and opaque nature of traditional payment tracking systems.

The ability to track the payment lifecycle empowers financial institutions with insights into the progress of transactions. This transparency is particularly valuable in scenarios where multiple parties are involved, each contributing to different phases of the payment process.

Instant Confirmation of Settlement: One of the revolutionary aspects of xCurrent's end-to-end tracking is the instant confirmation of settlement. Traditional correspondent banking models often involve delays in settlement confirmation, leading to uncertainties and potential risks. xCurrent eliminates this ambiguity by providing instant confirmation when a payment is successfully settled.

Financial institutions leveraging xCurrent can rely on real-time settlement confirmations, reducing exposure to settlement risks and enhancing the overall efficiency of cross-border payments. This instantaneous feedback loop contributes to a more secure and reliable payment ecosystem.

Reduction of Payment Reconciliation Efforts: The end-to-end tracking facilitated by xCurrent significantly reduces the need for extensive payment reconciliation efforts. In traditional correspondent banking, discrepancies and delays often necessitate manual reconciliation processes, leading to increased operational costs and potential errors.

xCurrent's tracking capabilities streamline the reconciliation process by providing a synchronized view of the payment journey. Financial institutions can confidently reconcile transactions based on the real-time data available, minimizing the need for labor-intensive and time-consuming reconciliation efforts.

Case Studies Illustrating Enhanced Payment Tracking:

Examining real-world case studies provides tangible examples of how xCurrent's capabilities in sending payment information and enabling end-to-end tracking impact the efficiency and transparency of cross-border payments.

Enhancing Visibility with Santander: Santander, a global banking giant, implemented xCurrent to enhance the visibility of cross-border payments for its customers. By leveraging xCurrent's real-time communication and end-to-end tracking features, Santander provided customers with unprecedented transparency into the status of their international transactions.

The implementation of xCurrent reduced the reliance on manual inquiry processes, as customers could track their payments in real-time through Santander's digital platforms. This enhanced visibility contributed to a positive customer experience and positioned Santander as a leader in providing transparent and efficient cross-border payment services.

Improving Settlement Efficiency with SBI Holdings: SBI Holdings, a financial services conglomerate based in Japan, collaborated with Ripple to improve settlement efficiency in cross-border payments. By adopting xCurrent, SBI Holdings enhanced its ability to track payments in real-time, reducing settlement times and minimizing operational complexities.

The improved settlement efficiency achieved through xCurrent's tracking capabilities allowed SBI Holdings to optimize its cross-border payment services. Customers experienced faster and more reliable transactions, contributing to SBI Holdings' reputation as a forward-thinking financial institution embracing innovative solutions.

Challenges and Considerations in Payment Tracking:

While xCurrent's capabilities in sending payment information and enabling end-to-end tracking bring about transformative advantages, certain challenges and considerations merit attention.

Integration with Legacy Systems: Integrating xCurrent into existing banking infrastructure may pose challenges for some financial institutions. Compatibility with legacy systems, data migration considerations, and the need for staff training are factors that institutions must carefully navigate to ensure a seamless transition.

The collaborative approach between xCurrent and financial institutions involves active engagement to address integration challenges and foster a smooth adoption process.

Privacy and Security Concerns: Real-time communication and end-to-end tracking raise privacy and security concerns that must be adequately addressed. Financial institutions need to implement robust security measures to protect sensitive payment information and ensure compliance with data protection regulations.

Collaborative efforts in privacy and security considerations involve ongoing dialogue between technology providers and financial institutions to stay ahead of evolving cybersecurity threats and regulatory requirements.

Interoperability with Diverse Systems: As financial institutions operate within a diverse landscape of payment systems and ledgers, ensuring interoperability is crucial. xCurrent's success in providing seamless communication relies on its ability to interoperate with a wide range of systems, protocols, and ledgers.

Collaborative efforts in interoperability involve ongoing updates and enhancements to xCurrent's capabilities, ensuring that it remains compatible with the evolving landscape of financial technologies.

Conclusion: Transforming Cross-Border Payments Through Transparency:

xCurrent's ability to send payment information and enable end-to-end tracking represents a pivotal advancement in the quest for transparency and efficiency in cross-border payments. As financial institutions embrace the capabilities of xCurrent, they move away from the opaque and fragmented nature of traditional correspondent banking, ushering in a new era where payments can be tracked in real-time from initiation to settlement.

As we progress through subsequent chapters, we will further explore the multifaceted impact of xCurrent on cross-border payments. From mitigating risks to improving compliance and fostering a more collaborative ecosystem, xCurrent's role extends beyond communication and tracking to shape the future of value transfer on a global scale.

No Need to Move Funds Between Ledgers

In the realm of cross-border payments, the traditional movement of funds between ledgers has long been a cumbersome and costly process. xCurrent, a pivotal component of Ripple's suite of solutions, challenges this paradigm by leveraging the Interledger Protocol (ILP) to enable communication between disparate ledgers without the necessity of physically moving funds. This chapter delves into the transformative subtopic of "No Need to Move Funds Between Ledgers," exploring how xCurrent reshapes cross-border transactions by eliminating the traditional complexities associated with fund movement.

Introduction to Ledger-to-Ledger Communication:

Before delving into the intricacies of eliminating the need to move funds between ledgers, it's crucial to understand the conventional challenges associated with cross-border fund movement and how xCurrent introduces a paradigm shift.

Traditional Fund Movement: Traditional cross-border payments typically involve the physical movement of funds between the ledgers of sending and receiving financial institutions. This process is often characterized by delays, high operational costs, and the need for pre-funded accounts to facilitate swift settlement. The movement of funds across different currencies and ledgers adds layers of complexity, creating inefficiencies that xCurrent seeks to address.

xCurrent's Approach: xCurrent disrupts the traditional fund movement model by introducing ledger-to-ledger communication facilitated by the Interledger Protocol. Instead of physically moving funds, xCurrent ensures that relevant information is communicated seamlessly between the ledgers of participating financial institutions. This approach not only expedites settlement but also reduces the need for pre-funded accounts and minimizes operational complexities.

The Significance of No Need to Move Funds Between Ledgers:

Eliminating the requirement to physically move funds between ledgers represents a paradigm shift in the cross-border payments landscape. This shift brings about several transformative advantages that contribute to the efficiency, transparency, and cost-effectiveness of cross-border transactions.

Instantaneous Settlement: One of the primary benefits of eliminating the need to move funds between ledgers is the potential for instantaneous settlement. Traditional cross-border payments often involve multi-day settlement periods due to the movement of funds across different banking systems and corresponding banks. xCurrent's ledger-to-ledger communication expedites settlement by transmitting relevant information in real-time, allowing for nearly instantaneous confirmation and finalization of transactions.

The instantaneous settlement introduced by xCurrent not only enhances the overall speed of cross-border payments but also contributes to a more predictable and reliable payment ecosystem. Financial institutions and end-users can experience the benefits of near-instant settlement, reducing uncertainties associated with traditional payment models.

Cost Reduction Through Pre-Funding Elimination: Traditional cross-border payments often require financial institutions to hold pre-funded accounts in various currencies to facilitate swift settlement. This practice ties up capital and leads to opportunity costs associated with idle funds. xCurrent's approach eliminates the need for pre-funded accounts by enabling ledger-to-ledger communication, resulting in significant cost reductions for participating financial institutions.

By removing the requirement for pre-funding, xCurrent allows financial institutions to optimize their capital allocation, directing resources toward growth initiatives rather than maintaining extensive reserves for cross-border settlements. The cost reduction achieved through the elimination of pre-funding contributes to a more efficient and financially sustainable cross-border payment ecosystem.

Enhanced Operational Efficiency: The elimination of the need to move funds between ledgers streamlines the entire cross-border payment process, leading to enhanced operational efficiency. Traditional correspondent banking models often involve a series of manual interventions, reconciliations, and delays associated with the movement of funds. xCurrent's ledger-to-ledger communication automates and accelerates these processes, reducing the reliance on manual interventions and minimizing operational complexities.

Financial institutions leveraging xCurrent experience a more streamlined and efficient cross-border payment workflow. The automation of settlement processes enhances overall operational efficiency, allowing institutions to allocate resources more strategically and focus on delivering improved services to their customers.

Ledger-to-Ledger Communication Workflow:

Understanding the workflow of ledger-to-ledger communication is integral to appreciating how xCurrent eliminates the need to move funds between ledgers and facilitates near-instant settlement in cross-border payments.

Payment Initiation: The process begins with the initiation of a cross-border payment by the sending financial institution. Using xCurrent, the institution transmits the relevant payment details to the receiving financial institution, including information such as the originator, beneficiary, transaction amount, and any regulatory or compliance requirements.

Ledger-to-Ledger Communication: Instead of physically moving funds, xCurrent facilitates ledger-to-ledger communication between the sending and receiving financial institutions. The Interledger Protocol acts as the communication bridge, allowing for the seamless transmission of payment information without the need for a direct connection between the ledgers.

During this phase, xCurrent ensures that both ledgers remain synchronized with the latest payment information. The transparency and real-time nature of ledger-to-ledger communication contribute to a shared understanding of the transaction status between the participating institutions.

Settlement Confirmation: Upon successful verification and agreement on the payment details, xCurrent provides near-instant settlement confirmation. The receiving financial institution acknowledges the receipt of payment information, and the transaction is considered settled. This instantaneous settlement confirmation replaces the traditional model of waiting for funds to move across different banking systems and corresponding banks.

Post-Settlement Processes: Following settlement confirmation, xCurrent automates post-settlement processes, including reconciliation and reporting. The synchronized view of payment information on both ledgers minimizes the need for extensive reconciliation efforts, reducing operational complexities for financial institutions.

Benefits of Eliminating the Need to Move Funds Between Ledgers:

The transformative advantages brought about by xCurrent's elimination of the need to move funds between ledgers extend across various dimensions of cross-border payments.

Reduced Settlement Risks: Traditional cross-border payments are often exposed to settlement risks associated with delays, errors, or uncertainties in the movement of funds. By eliminating the physical movement of funds, xCurrent significantly reduces settlement risks. The instantaneous settlement confirmation ensures that financial institutions can rely on the timely finalization of transactions, minimizing exposure to potential risks.

Reduced settlement risks contribute to a more secure and reliable cross-border payment ecosystem, fostering trust among financial institutions and end-users.

Improved Liquidity Management: The elimination of the need for pre-funded accounts results in improved liquidity management for financial institutions. xCurrent's ledger-to-ledger communication allows institutions to dynamically allocate liquidity precisely when and where it is needed for settlement. This optimization aligns with broader strategic goals, enabling financial institutions to deploy resources more efficiently and supporting initiatives such as innovation, expansion into new markets, or investment in technology.

Improved liquidity management represents a fundamental shift in the way financial institutions approach cross-border payments, moving away from static pre-funding models to a more dynamic and responsive liquidity framework.

Enhanced Cross-Border Payment Speed: The near-instantaneous settlement made possible by xCurrent's elimination of the need to move funds between ledgers contributes to enhanced cross-border payment speed. Traditional models involving fund movement across different banking systems and corresponding banks can result in multi-day settlement periods. xCurrent's ledger-to-ledger communication reduces settlement times to near-instant, providing financial institutions and end-users with swift and reliable cross-border transactions.

Enhanced cross-border payment speed aligns with the expectations of a rapidly evolving digital economy, where efficiency and immediacy are key factors in meeting customer demands.

Case Studies Illustrating the Impact of Eliminating Fund Movement:

Examining real-world case studies provides tangible examples of how xCurrent's approach of eliminating the need to move funds between ledgers transforms the efficiency and cost-effectiveness of cross-border payments.

Optimizing Capital Allocation with Standard Chartered: Standard Chartered, a global banking institution, leveraged xCurrent to optimize its capital allocation for cross-border payments. By eliminating the need for pre-funded accounts and enabling ledger-to-ledger communication, Standard Chartered reduced the capital tied up in idle reserves and directed resources toward strategic initiatives.

The optimization of capital allocation contributed to Standard Chartered's ability to operate more efficiently in the cross-border payment landscape. The institution could deploy resources dynamically, supporting its growth objectives and enhancing its competitive positioning.

Expediting Settlement with Axis Bank: Axis Bank, a leading financial institution in India, adopted xCurrent to expedite cross-border settlement processes. The elimination of the need to move funds between ledgers allowed Axis Bank to provide its customers with near-instant settlement confirmation, reducing the time and uncertainties associated with traditional cross-border payment models.

The expedited settlement achieved through xCurrent contributed to Axis Bank's reputation for delivering reliable and efficient cross-border payment services, attracting customers seeking a seamless and timely international transaction experience.

Challenges and Considerations in Eliminating Fund Movement:

While xCurrent's elimination of the need to move funds between ledgers brings about transformative advantages, certain challenges and considerations merit attention.

Integration Complexity: Integrating xCurrent into existing banking infrastructure may pose challenges related to compatibility with legacy systems, data migration considerations, and the need for staff training. The collaborative approach between xCurrent and financial institutions involves active engagement to address integration challenges and foster a smooth adoption process.

Regulatory Compliance: Ensuring regulatory compliance remains a critical consideration in the context of cross-border payments. Collaborative efforts between xCurrent and financial institutions involve proactive engagement with regulators to navigate evolving regulatory landscapes and establish a framework that aligns with compliance requirements.

Educational Initiatives: Educational initiatives play a vital role in overcoming challenges associated with the adoption of innovative solutions like xCurrent. Financial institutions may face challenges in ensuring that their staff and end-users have a comprehensive understanding of the benefits and mechanics of eliminating the need to move funds between ledgers.

Collaborative efforts in educational initiatives aim to bridge this knowledge gap and foster a shared understanding of the transformative potential of xCurrent in reshaping cross-border payments.

Conclusion: Reshaping Cross-Border Payments Through Ledger-to-Ledger Communication:

xCurrent's revolutionary approach of eliminating the need to move funds between ledgers represents a paradigm shift in the cross-border payments landscape. By leveraging ledger-to-ledger communication facilitated by the Interledger Protocol, xCurrent streamlines settlement processes, enhances transparency, and contributes to a more efficient and cost-effective cross-border payment ecosystem.

As we progress through subsequent chapters, we will further explore the multifaceted impact of xCurrent on cross-border payments. From enhancing transparency to reducing operational complexities and fostering a collaborative ecosystem, xCurrent's role extends beyond eliminating the need to move funds between ledgers to shape the future of value transfer on a global scale.

Integrates with Legacy Systems

In the ever-evolving landscape of cross-border payments, one of the significant challenges faced by financial institutions is the integration of innovative solutions with existing legacy systems. xCurrent, a cornerstone of Ripple's suite of solutions, addresses this challenge by offering seamless integration capabilities with legacy systems. This chapter explores the transformative subtopic of "Integrates with Legacy Systems," examining how xCurrent facilitates a smooth transition for financial institutions by harmonizing new technologies with established infrastructure.

Navigating the Legacy Landscape:

Before delving into the specifics of how xCurrent integrates with legacy systems, it's crucial to understand the complexities financial institutions face when dealing with legacy infrastructure in the context of cross-border payments.

Legacy Systems in Financial Institutions: Financial institutions often rely on legacy systems, which are long-established, often outdated, and deeply ingrained technology platforms. These legacy systems have been the backbone of banking operations for decades, handling various functions, including transaction processing, record-keeping, and compliance. However, they can pose challenges when adapting to the fast-paced evolution of modern payment technologies.

Challenges of Legacy Systems: Legacy systems are characterized by their rigidity, lack of interoperability, and resistance to rapid changes. These traits make it challenging for financial institutions to adopt and integrate new technologies seamlessly. In the context of cross-border payments, the need for real-time communication, transparency, and compliance with evolving regulatory standards requires a shift from traditional to more agile and interoperable systems.

The Role of xCurrent in Integration:

xCurrent emerges as a solution designed to bridge the gap between the traditional and the modern in the realm of cross-border payments. By offering integration capabilities with legacy systems, xCurrent becomes a key enabler for financial institutions looking to modernize their operations without undergoing a disruptive overhaul of their existing infrastructure.

Seamless Integration with Existing Systems: One of the pivotal features of xCurrent is its ability to seamlessly integrate with a variety of legacy systems. Financial institutions can incorporate xCurrent into their existing technology stack without the need for a complete overhaul. This seamless integration is facilitated by the flexibility and adaptability built into the design of xCurrent, allowing it to coexist with diverse legacy architectures.

Interoperability Across Platforms: xCurrent's interoperability is a crucial aspect of its integration capabilities. It is designed to communicate and transact across different platforms and systems, ensuring that financial institutions can maintain compatibility with their legacy infrastructure while still benefiting from the advanced features offered by xCurrent. This interoperability extends to various messaging protocols, data formats, and communication standards commonly used in the financial industry.

Preservation of Data and Processes: Integrating with legacy systems involves the preservation of existing data and business processes. xCurrent is designed to respect and work within the established data structures and workflows of financial institutions. This preservation ensures a smooth transition without disruption to critical functions, allowing financial institutions to leverage the advantages of xCurrent while retaining the integrity of their historical data and operational processes.

Integration Workflow:

Understanding the workflow of how xCurrent integrates with legacy systems provides insight into the collaborative and adaptive nature of this process.

Assessment and Compatibility Checks: The integration process begins with a comprehensive assessment of the existing legacy systems within a financial institution. This involves evaluating the technology stack, data structures, communication protocols, and the overall architecture. Compatibility checks are performed to ensure that xCurrent can seamlessly interface with the legacy systems without causing conflicts or disruptions.

Configuration and Customization: Once compatibility is established, xCurrent undergoes configuration and customization to align with the specific requirements of the financial institution. This may involve tailoring communication protocols, data mappings, and transaction workflows to integrate seamlessly with the legacy infrastructure. The flexibility of xCurrent allows for a high degree of customization, ensuring a harmonious fit with diverse legacy systems.

Integration Testing: A crucial phase in the integration process is thorough testing to validate the seamless interaction between xCurrent and the legacy systems. Integration testing includes scenarios that simulate real-world cross-border payment transactions, ensuring that data is accurately transmitted, processes are executed smoothly, and the integrated system performs reliably under various conditions.

Pilot Implementation: Before full-scale deployment, a pilot implementation may be conducted to validate the integration in a controlled environment. This allows financial institutions to observe how xCurrent functions in conjunction with their legacy systems in real-world scenarios with a limited impact on day-to-day operations.

Full-Scale Deployment: Upon successful completion of testing and pilot implementation, xCurrent is deployed at full scale across the financial institution's cross-border payment operations. The integrated system operates seamlessly, leveraging the strengths of xCurrent while working in harmony with existing legacy systems.

Benefits of Integration with Legacy Systems:

The integration of xCurrent with legacy systems brings forth a range of benefits that contribute to the efficiency, transparency, and adaptability of cross-border payments.

Preservation of Investments: Financial institutions have made significant investments in their legacy systems over the years. Integration with xCurrent allows them to preserve these investments by leveraging existing infrastructure while modernizing specific aspects of their cross-border payment operations. This approach represents a pragmatic and cost-effective strategy, avoiding the need for a complete technology overhaul.

Minimized Disruption to Operations: The seamless integration capabilities of xCurrent ensure that there is minimal disruption to day-to-day operations during the transition. Financial institutions can continue to conduct cross-border payments using their established workflows and processes, gradually incorporating the advanced features of xCurrent without undergoing a sudden and disruptive change.

Enhanced Data Security and Compliance: The preservation of existing data structures and processes ensures that sensitive information handled by legacy systems remains secure. xCurrent's integration is designed to align with data protection and compliance standards, providing financial institutions with the assurance that their cross-border payment operations meet regulatory requirements.

Adaptability to Changing Regulatory Standards: Financial regulations in the cross-border payments landscape are subject to frequent changes. xCurrent's integration capabilities allow financial institutions to adapt swiftly to evolving regulatory standards. The flexibility of xCurrent enables quick adjustments to compliance protocols, ensuring that financial institutions stay compliant with regulatory requirements.

Operational Efficiency and Automation: Integration with xCurrent introduces operational efficiency by automating various aspects of cross-border payment processes. Tasks that were traditionally manual and time-consuming, such as reconciliation and settlement, can be automated through xCurrent's advanced features. This automation leads to increased operational efficiency, reduced errors, and streamlined workflows.

Real-World Examples of Integration Success:

Examining real-world examples provides tangible illustrations of how financial institutions have successfully integrated xCurrent with their legacy systems to enhance cross-border payment capabilities.

Enhancing Efficiency with Banco Santander: Banco Santander, a global banking giant, integrated xCurrent with its legacy systems to enhance the efficiency of cross-border payments. The seamless integration allowed Banco Santander to leverage xCurrent's real-time communication and settlement features without disrupting existing banking operations.

The integration resulted in faster and more transparent cross-border payments for Banco Santander's customers. The bank could offer enhanced services without compromising its legacy infrastructure, showcasing the successful integration of xCurrent within an established banking ecosystem.

Modernizing Processes with SBI Holdings: SBI Holdings, a financial services conglomerate based in Japan, embraced xCurrent to modernize its cross-border payment processes. The integration with legacy systems enabled SBI Holdings to enhance its capabilities in tracking payments, reducing settlement times, and optimizing liquidity management.

SBI Holdings achieved a successful integration that aligned with its strategic objectives. The company's cross-border payment services evolved to meet the demands of a rapidly changing financial landscape while maintaining compatibility with its legacy infrastructure.

Challenges and Considerations in Integration:

While the integration of xCurrent with legacy systems brings about numerous benefits, certain challenges and considerations should be addressed during the implementation process.

Compatibility with Diverse Systems: Financial institutions operate diverse legacy systems, each with its unique architecture and technology stack. Ensuring compatibility with this diversity can be a complex task. Collaborative efforts between financial institutions and the development team behind xCurrent involve comprehensive compatibility testing and the development of adaptable interfaces to accommodate different legacy environments.

Data Migration and Mapping: The integration process may require data migration and mapping to align existing data structures with xCurrent's requirements. This task involves careful planning and execution to avoid data discrepancies or loss during the transition. Financial institutions and the xCurrent development team collaborate to define data mapping strategies and ensure a seamless transfer of information.

Staff Training and Adoption: Integrating xCurrent introduces new features and functionalities that may require staff training and adoption. Financial institutions must invest in educational initiatives to familiarize their staff with the capabilities of xCurrent and ensure a smooth transition to the integrated system. User-friendly interfaces and documentation play a crucial role in facilitating the adoption process.

Regulatory Alignment: Adhering to regulatory standards is a paramount consideration in the integration of xCurrent with legacy systems. Financial institutions must collaborate with regulatory authorities to ensure that the integrated system complies with evolving standards. This collaborative approach involves ongoing communication and updates to adapt to changing regulatory landscapes.

Conclusion: Harmonizing the Future with the Past in Cross-Border Payments:

xCurrent's ability to integrate seamlessly with legacy systems marks a significant advancement in the evolution of cross-border payments. By offering a bridge between traditional infrastructure and modern technologies, xCurrent enables financial institutions to embrace the future without abandoning their past investments. As we progress through subsequent chapters, we will continue to explore the multifaceted impact of xCurrent on cross-border payments, unveiling how this integration paves the way for a more interconnected, efficient, and transparent global payment ecosystem.

Provides Transparency into Global Payments

In the intricate landscape of cross-border payments, transparency has been a longstanding challenge. The lack of real-time visibility into the movement and status of funds has led to inefficiencies, delays, and increased operational costs. xCurrent, a pivotal component of Ripple's suite of solutions, emerges as a transformative force by providing transparency into global payments. This chapter delves into the subtopic of "Provides Transparency into Global Payments," exploring how xCurrent reshapes the cross-border payment narrative by offering a real-time view of transactions and enhancing visibility for financial institutions.

The Quest for Transparency in Cross-Border Payments:

Before delving into the specifics of how xCurrent provides transparency, it's essential to understand the historical challenges associated with achieving transparency in cross-border payments.

Opaque Nature of Traditional Cross-Border Payments: Traditional cross-border payment systems are characterized by their opaque and fragmented nature. Financial institutions involved in correspondent banking often face challenges in obtaining real-time information about the status and location of funds during the settlement process. This lack of transparency introduces uncertainties, reconciliation complexities, and delays in cross-border transactions.

Operational Challenges: The absence of transparency poses operational challenges for financial institutions, including difficulties in tracking payment flows, reconciling ledgers, and responding to customer inquiries promptly. These challenges not only impact the efficiency of cross-border payments but also contribute to increased costs and a less-than-optimal customer experience.

Empowering Financial Institutions with Real-Time Visibility:

xCurrent addresses the historical challenges of transparency in cross-border payments by providing financial institutions with real-time visibility into the entire payment process. This section explores the key mechanisms through which xCurrent achieves transparency and the transformative impact on global payments.

Instant Payment Status Updates: One of the foundational features of xCurrent is its ability to provide instant payment status updates. Financial institutions leveraging xCurrent can access real-time information about the status of cross-border transactions. This includes details such as whether a payment has been initiated, its current location in the settlement process, and the expected time of completion.

The provision of instant payment status updates revolutionizes the traditional cross-border payment experience, allowing financial institutions to make informed decisions, manage customer expectations, and enhance overall operational efficiency.

End-to-End Transaction Visibility: xCurrent facilitates end-to-end transaction visibility by offering a comprehensive view of the payment journey from initiation to settlement. This transparency extends across the entire network of financial institutions participating in the transaction. Each participant gains visibility into the transaction's progress, ensuring a synchronized understanding of the payment status.

End-to-end transaction visibility mitigates the challenges associated with fragmented payment information, reducing the need for manual interventions and streamlining the reconciliation process. Financial institutions can collaborate more effectively, confident in their shared understanding of the payment lifecycle.

Tracking and Confirmation Features: xCurrent incorporates robust tracking and confirmation features that empower financial institutions to track the movement of funds in real-time. This includes tracking the funds' path through various intermediary banks and confirming their arrival at the destination institution.

The tracking and confirmation features enhance transparency by providing a granular view of the payment route and milestones achieved. Financial institutions can proactively address any issues that may arise during the payment journey, reducing the likelihood of delays and ensuring a smoother cross-border payment experience.

Transaction Status Notifications: xCurrent enables the automatic generation of transaction status notifications, keeping all relevant parties informed about the progress of cross-border payments. These notifications can be customized based on the preferences of the participating financial institutions, ensuring that key stakeholders receive timely updates.

Transaction status notifications contribute to transparency by fostering proactive communication among financial institutions. This real-time communication streamlines the resolution of potential issues, reduces uncertainties, and enhances the overall reliability of cross-border payments.

Benefits of Transparency in Global Payments:

The transparency introduced by xCurrent brings forth a myriad of benefits for financial institutions engaged in cross-border payments. This section explores these benefits and the positive impact on operational efficiency, risk mitigation, and customer satisfaction.

Operational Efficiency: Transparency contributes significantly to operational efficiency in cross-border payments. Financial institutions can optimize their workflows, reduce manual interventions, and streamline reconciliation processes when armed with real-time visibility into payment status and transaction details.

By minimizing the time spent on resolving discrepancies and addressing payment-related issues, financial institutions can allocate resources more strategically, improving overall operational efficiency.

Risk Mitigation: The real-time visibility provided by xCurrent plays a crucial role in risk mitigation. Financial institutions can identify and address potential issues as they arise, reducing the likelihood of delays, errors, or disputes. Timely information about the payment status allows for proactive risk management, contributing to a more secure and reliable cross-border payment ecosystem.

Reduced settlement risks, increased compliance with regulatory standards, and improved fraud detection are among the risk mitigation benefits facilitated by the transparency introduced by xCurrent.

Enhanced Customer Satisfaction: Transparency into the cross-border payment process directly impacts customer satisfaction. xCurrent's ability to provide instant payment status updates and transaction visibility empowers financial institutions to offer a more transparent and predictable experience to their customers.

Customers benefit from the ability to track their payments in real-time, receive timely updates, and gain assurance about the reliability of cross-border transactions. Enhanced customer satisfaction contributes to brand loyalty and strengthens the competitive position of financial institutions in the market.

Cost Reduction: The transparency introduced by xCurrent contributes to cost reduction in cross-border payments. Operational efficiencies, risk mitigation, and enhanced customer satisfaction collectively lead to a more cost-effective payment ecosystem. Financial institutions can allocate resources more efficiently, reduce the need for extensive manual interventions, and avoid costs associated with delays or disputes.

By minimizing the complexities and uncertainties inherent in traditional cross-border payments, xCurrent paves the way for a streamlined and cost-effective global payment infrastructure.

Real-World Examples of Transparency Impact:

Examining real-world examples provides tangible illustrations of how financial institutions have benefited from the transparency introduced by xCurrent in their cross-border payment operations.

Improving Customer Experience with PNC: PNC, a prominent financial institution in the United States, integrated xCurrent to enhance transparency in its cross-border payment processes. The real-time visibility provided by xCurrent allowed PNC to offer improved customer experiences by providing instant payment status updates and transaction visibility.

Customers of PNC could track the progress of their cross-border payments, receive timely notifications, and experience a more transparent and predictable payment journey. The enhanced customer experience contributed to PNC's reputation for delivering reliable and customer-centric cross-border payment services.

Optimizing Operations with Standard Chartered: Standard Chartered, a global banking institution, leveraged xCurrent to optimize its cross-border payment operations. The transparency introduced by xCurrent allowed Standard Chartered to streamline its workflows, reduce manual interventions, and enhance overall operational efficiency.

The optimization of operations resulted in cost savings for Standard Chartered, highlighting how transparency contributes to a more efficient and economically sustainable cross-border payment ecosystem.

Challenges and Considerations in Providing Transparency:

While xCurrent enhances transparency in cross-border payments, certain challenges and considerations should be acknowledged to ensure successful implementation and operation.

Data Privacy and Security: The transparency facilitated by xCurrent involves the exchange of real-time information among financial institutions. Ensuring the privacy and security of sensitive data during this exchange is paramount. Collaborative efforts between financial institutions and the developers of xCurrent involve robust data protection measures and adherence to privacy standards.

Regulatory Compliance: Transparency initiatives must align with regulatory standards and compliance requirements. Financial institutions leveraging xCurrent work collaboratively with regulators to ensure that the transparency features meet evolving regulatory expectations. Proactive engagement with regulatory authorities ensures that the transparency introduced by xCurrent is compliant with the dynamic landscape of financial regulations.

Integration with Existing Systems: Providing transparency through xCurrent requires seamless integration with existing systems. Compatibility with diverse legacy systems, data mapping considerations, and interoperability challenges may be encountered during the integration process. Financial institutions and the development team behind xCurrent collaborate to address these challenges and ensure a smooth integration that aligns with existing infrastructure.

Conclusion: Illuminating the Future of Cross-Border Payments:

xCurrent's transformative impact on cross-border payments extends beyond facilitating transactions—it illuminates the global payment landscape with unprecedented transparency. By offering real-time visibility, end-to-end transaction tracking, and instant payment status updates, xCurrent empowers financial institutions to navigate the complexities of cross-border payments with confidence. As we progress through subsequent chapters, we will continue to explore how the transparency introduced by xCurrent reshapes the dynamics of global payments, fostering a more connected, efficient, and secure cross-border payment ecosystem.

Chapter 4: xVia - A Standard API for Payments
Single Connection to Payment Providers Globally

In the dynamic landscape of cross-border payments, achieving seamless connectivity with diverse payment providers worldwide has been a longstanding challenge. xVia, a pivotal component of Ripple's suite of solutions, addresses this challenge by serving as a standard API for payments. This chapter explores the transformative subtopic of "Single Connection to Payment Providers Globally," delving into how xVia simplifies the complex web of connections, offering financial institutions a unified interface to access a global network of payment providers.

The Complexity of Global Payment Connectivity:

Before exploring the role of xVia, it's crucial to understand the complexities associated with establishing connections to payment providers on a global scale.

Diverse Ecosystem of Payment Providers: Financial institutions engaged in cross-border payments interact with a diverse ecosystem of payment providers, each with its unique technology infrastructure, communication protocols, and data formats. This diversity poses challenges for financial institutions aiming to establish and maintain connections with a multitude of payment service providers globally.

Fragmented Communication Protocols: The payment industry is characterized by the use of fragmented communication protocols, making it challenging for financial institutions to create standardized interfaces that can seamlessly interact with various payment providers. The lack of a unified standard often leads to inefficiencies, increased development efforts, and complexities in managing multiple connections.

Empowering Financial Institutions with xVia:

xVia emerges as a solution designed to simplify the complexities of global payment connectivity. By offering a standard API for payments, xVia enables financial institutions to establish a single connection that grants access to a global network of payment providers. This section explores the key features and mechanisms through which xVia streamlines global payment connectivity.

Unified Interface for Payment Providers: At the core of xVia's functionality is its provision of a unified interface for payment providers. Financial institutions can connect to xVia through a standardized API, eliminating the need to develop and maintain custom integrations for each payment service provider individually.

The unified interface abstracts the complexities of interacting with diverse payment providers, providing financial institutions with a streamlined and standardized way to send and receive payments globally. This abstraction layer significantly reduces the development efforts required to establish and maintain connections, fostering operational efficiency.

Standardized Data Formats: xVia employs standardized data formats to ensure compatibility with a wide range of payment providers. Financial institutions can send payment instructions to xVia using a standardized data structure, and xVia takes care of translating and formatting the data according to the requirements of the destination payment provider.

This standardization simplifies the integration process for financial institutions, as they no longer need to adapt their systems to accommodate the varied data formats used by different payment service providers. xVia acts as a universal translator, ensuring seamless communication across the global payment network.

Protocol Agnosticism: Recognizing the diversity of communication protocols used by payment providers, xVia operates as a protocol-agnostic solution. Financial institutions can connect to xVia using their preferred communication protocol, and xVia translates and communicates with payment providers using the respective protocols they support.

This protocol agnosticism eliminates the need for financial institutions to invest in specialized infrastructure to accommodate different protocols. xVia serves as a flexible gateway that adapts to the unique requirements of each payment provider, ensuring a harmonious and interoperable global payment network.

Comprehensive Connectivity: xVia provides comprehensive connectivity by offering access to a broad network of payment providers across different regions and financial ecosystems. Financial institutions leveraging xVia gain the ability to send payments to beneficiaries in diverse geographic locations through a single connection.

This comprehensive connectivity is particularly advantageous for financial institutions with a global footprint or those seeking to expand their reach. xVia acts as a gateway that opens doors to a multitude of payment corridors, simplifying the complexities of establishing and maintaining connections in various regions.

Benefits of Single Connection to Payment Providers:

The single connection to payment providers facilitated by xVia brings forth a range of benefits for financial institutions engaged in cross-border payments. This section explores these benefits and the positive impact on operational efficiency, cost-effectiveness, and scalability.

Operational Efficiency: Simplifying the process of connecting to payment providers globally significantly enhances operational efficiency for financial institutions. The unified interface provided by xVia reduces the complexities associated with managing multiple integrations, minimizing the need for custom development efforts.

Financial institutions can focus on optimizing their payment workflows and providing enhanced services to their customers, leveraging the streamlined connectivity facilitated by xVia. This operational efficiency translates to quicker time-to-market for new services and increased agility in responding to evolving market demands.

Cost-Effectiveness: Establishing and maintaining connections with a diverse array of payment providers can be resource-intensive. The single connection to payment providers offered by xVia contributes to cost-effectiveness by reducing development and maintenance costs associated with managing multiple integrations.

Financial institutions benefit from economies of scale as they leverage a standardized API and data format for interactions with payment providers. The cost savings achieved through xVia's streamlined connectivity allow financial institutions to allocate resources strategically, driving economic sustainability in their cross-border payment operations.

Scalability and Rapid Expansion: xVia's comprehensive connectivity enables financial institutions to scale their cross-border payment operations rapidly. As they can access a global network of payment providers through a single connection, expanding into new regions or corridors becomes a streamlined process.

Financial institutions can explore new business opportunities, enter emerging markets, and serve a broader customer base without the constraints of managing intricate integrations for each payment corridor. The scalability provided by xVia empowers financial institutions to adapt to changing market dynamics and grow their cross-border payment services organically.

Reduced Development Time: Custom integrations with payment providers often require significant development time and effort. xVia reduces development time by offering a standardized API and eliminating the need for financial institutions to tailor their systems to the unique requirements of each payment provider.

The reduced development time accelerates the implementation of new payment services, product enhancements, and system upgrades. Financial institutions can bring innovations to market more swiftly, staying ahead of competition and meeting the evolving needs of their customers.

Real-World Examples of Single Connection Success:

Examining real-world examples provides tangible illustrations of how financial institutions have benefited from xVia's single connection to payment providers in their cross-border payment operations.

Streamlining Connectivity with BBVA: BBVA, a leading global financial institution, leveraged xVia to streamline its connectivity with payment providers worldwide. By adopting xVia's standardized API, BBVA simplified the integration process and reduced the complexities associated with managing multiple connections.

The streamlined connectivity enabled BBVA to enhance its operational efficiency, offer a broader range of cross-border payment services, and enter new markets with ease. The success of BBVA's integration with xVia showcased the transformative impact of a single connection to payment providers.

Expanding Payment Corridors with Siam Commercial Bank: Siam Commercial Bank (SCB), a prominent financial institution in Thailand, utilized xVia to expand its payment corridors and provide seamless cross-border payment services. xVia's comprehensive connectivity allowed SCB to establish connections with payment providers in key regions, facilitating international transactions for its customers.

The ability to rapidly expand payment corridors through a single connection empowered SCB to serve a broader customer base and strengthen its position in the competitive cross-border payment landscape. The success of SCB's integration highlighted the scalability and efficiency achieved with xVia.

Challenges and Considerations in Single Connection:

While xVia simplifies the complexities of global payment connectivity, certain challenges and considerations should be addressed to ensure successful implementation and operation.

Customization Requirements: Financial institutions may have unique customization requirements based on their specific business processes or regulatory environments. While xVia offers a standardized API, it's essential to consider the flexibility and customization options available to accommodate these specific requirements. Collaborative efforts between financial institutions and the development team behind xVia involve defining customization parameters to align with individual needs.

Integration with Internal Systems: Integrating xVia with internal systems, including existing payment platforms and back-office infrastructure, requires careful planning. Financial institutions need to ensure a seamless integration that aligns with their internal workflows and processes. Collaborative efforts during the integration process involve mapping data flows, aligning with existing system architectures, and ensuring minimal disruption to ongoing operations.

Security and Compliance: Ensuring the security of data transmitted through a single connection and compliance with regulatory standards are paramount considerations. Financial institutions and the developers of xVia collaborate to implement robust security measures, including encryption protocols and adherence to industry and regulatory standards. Proactive engagement with regulatory authorities ensures that the single connection provided by xVia aligns with evolving compliance requirements.

Conclusion: Forging a Unified Future in Cross-Border Payments:

xVia's role as a standard API for payments brings forth a unified future in cross-border payments, simplifying the intricate web of connections that financial institutions navigate. By offering a single connection to payment providers globally, xVia empowers financial institutions to transcend the complexities of varied communication protocols and diverse ecosystems. As we progress through subsequent chapters, we will continue to explore how xVia reshapes the landscape of cross-border payments, unlocking new possibilities for efficiency, scalability, and innovation.

Abstraction Layer over RippleNet

In the intricate realm of cross-border payments, the need for a simplified and standardized interface that transcends the complexities of varied financial systems and networks is paramount. xVia, an integral component of Ripple's suite of solutions, serves as a standard API for payments, offering financial institutions an abstraction layer over RippleNet. This chapter explores the transformative subtopic of "Abstraction Layer over RippleNet," delving into how xVia acts as a unifying force, abstracting complexities and providing a seamless interface for financial institutions to interact with RippleNet.

Understanding the Role of Abstraction Layers:

Before exploring the specificities of xVia's abstraction layer over RippleNet, it's crucial to grasp the concept of abstraction layers and their significance in the context of cross-border payments.

Abstraction in Software Development: In software development, an abstraction layer is a way of hiding the intricate details of the underlying system or infrastructure, presenting a simplified and standardized interface for interacting with that system. Abstraction layers serve as a bridge, allowing developers or users to interact with complex systems without needing to understand the intricacies of the internal workings.

Importance of Abstraction in Payments: In the domain of cross-border payments, where diverse financial systems, protocols, and networks coexist, the importance of abstraction cannot be overstated. Financial institutions often grapple with the challenge of navigating the complexities of various payment networks, each with its unique features and protocols. Abstraction layers simplify this process, providing a standardized interface that streamlines interactions.

Empowering Financial Institutions with xVia's Abstraction Layer:

xVia's abstraction layer over RippleNet is designed to empower financial institutions by providing a unified and simplified interface for interacting with the RippleNet ecosystem. This section explores the key features and mechanisms through which xVia's abstraction layer abstracts complexities, offering financial institutions a seamless gateway to RippleNet.

Standardized Interaction with RippleNet: At the core of xVia's abstraction layer is its ability to provide a standardized interaction interface with RippleNet. Financial institutions can connect to xVia through a standardized API, abstracting the intricacies of RippleNet's internal operations. This standardized interface ensures that financial institutions, regardless of their internal systems or technology stacks, can seamlessly integrate with RippleNet.

The standardized interaction streamlines the integration process, reducing the complexities associated with adapting to the specific features of RippleNet. Financial institutions gain the flexibility to focus on optimizing their payment workflows rather than investing resources in custom integrations.

Seamless Integration with Internal Systems: xVia's abstraction layer facilitates seamless integration with a financial institution's internal systems. By abstracting the complexities of RippleNet, xVia ensures that the integration process aligns with the existing workflows and processes of the financial institution. This seamless integration allows financial institutions to leverage the benefits of RippleNet without disrupting their internal operations.

During the integration process, financial institutions collaborate with the development team behind xVia to map data flows, align with existing system architectures, and ensure minimal disruption to ongoing operations. The abstraction layer acts as a harmonizing force, enabling a smooth and efficient integration experience.

Adaptability to Diverse Technology Stacks: Recognizing the diversity of technology stacks employed by different financial institutions, xVia's abstraction layer is designed to be adaptable. Financial institutions can connect to xVia using their preferred programming languages, communication protocols, and technology infrastructure. xVia then abstracts these diverse elements, ensuring compatibility with the internal systems of each financial institution.

This adaptability is crucial for financial institutions with varied technology stacks, allowing them to integrate with RippleNet without the need for extensive modifications to their existing infrastructure. xVia's abstraction layer acts as a bridge that accommodates the unique requirements of each financial institution.

Protocol Agnosticism: Similar to xVia's role in providing a single connection to payment providers, its abstraction layer over RippleNet operates as protocol-agnostic. Financial institutions can interact with xVia using their preferred communication protocols, and xVia takes care of translating and communicating with RippleNet using the protocols it supports.

This protocol-agnostic approach eliminates the need for financial institutions to invest in specialized infrastructure to accommodate different protocols within RippleNet. xVia serves as a flexible gateway that adapts to the unique requirements of RippleNet, ensuring harmonious and interoperable interactions.

Benefits of Abstraction Layer over RippleNet:

The abstraction layer provided by xVia over RippleNet yields a range of benefits for financial institutions engaged in cross-border payments. This section explores these benefits and the positive impact on operational efficiency, adaptability, and scalability.

Operational Efficiency: One of the primary benefits of xVia's abstraction layer is the enhancement of operational efficiency for financial institutions. By providing a standardized and seamless interface for interaction with RippleNet, xVia reduces the complexities associated with navigating the internal workings of RippleNet.

Financial institutions can focus on optimizing their payment workflows and providing enhanced services to their customers, leveraging the streamlined connectivity facilitated by xVia. The abstraction layer contributes to quicker time-to-market for new services, increased agility in responding to market demands, and overall operational excellence.

Adaptability to Varied Infrastructures: The adaptability offered by xVia's abstraction layer is instrumental for financial institutions with varied technology infrastructures. Regardless of the programming languages, communication protocols, or technology stacks used internally, financial institutions can seamlessly integrate with RippleNet through xVia's standardized interface.

This adaptability ensures that financial institutions can leverage the benefits of RippleNet without significant modifications to their existing infrastructure. It allows for a flexible and accommodating integration process that aligns with the unique characteristics of each financial institution.

Reduced Development Time: Custom integrations with complex systems like RippleNet often require significant development time and effort. xVia's abstraction layer reduces development time by offering a standardized API and eliminating the need for financial institutions to tailor their systems to the intricacies of RippleNet.

The reduced development time accelerates the implementation of new payment services, product enhancements, and system upgrades. Financial institutions can bring innovations to market more swiftly, staying ahead of competition and meeting the evolving needs of their customers.

Scalability and Future-Proofing: The abstraction layer provided by xVia contributes to the scalability of cross-border payment operations for financial institutions. As they can interact with RippleNet through a standardized interface, financial institutions can scale their operations more rapidly and efficiently.

This scalability ensures that financial institutions are well-positioned to adapt to changing market dynamics, enter new markets, and explore emerging opportunities without the constraints of intricate integrations. The abstraction layer serves as a future-proofing mechanism, allowing financial institutions to evolve in tandem with advancements in the cross-border payments landscape.

Real-World Examples of Abstraction Layer Success:

Examining real-world examples provides tangible illustrations of how financial institutions have benefited from xVia's abstraction layer over RippleNet in their cross-border payment operations.

Simplifying Integration with American Express: American Express, a global financial services company, leveraged xVia's abstraction layer to simplify its integration with RippleNet. The standardized interface provided by xVia allowed American Express to seamlessly connect its internal systems with RippleNet, reducing the complexities associated with custom integrations.

The simplified integration empowered American Express to explore new cross-border payment services, optimize its operational workflows, and provide enhanced services to its customers. The success of American Express's integration showcased the transformative impact of xVia's abstraction layer.

Enhancing Connectivity with Santander: Santander, a prominent global banking institution, utilized xVia's abstraction layer to enhance its connectivity with RippleNet. By adopting xVia's standardized API, Santander streamlined its integration process, abstracting the complexities of RippleNet's internal operations.

The enhanced connectivity enabled Santander to offer a broader range of cross-border payment services, improve its operational efficiency, and strengthen its competitive position. Santander's success highlighted the adaptability and operational benefits achieved with xVia's abstraction layer.

Challenges and Considerations in Abstraction Layer Implementation:

While xVia's abstraction layer simplifies the integration process with RippleNet, certain challenges and considerations should be addressed to ensure successful implementation and operation.

Mapping Data Flows: Mapping data flows between a financial institution's internal systems and RippleNet is a critical aspect of the integration process. Collaborative efforts between financial institutions and the development team behind xVia involve defining and aligning data flows to ensure seamless communication and data exchange.

Ensuring a comprehensive understanding of data flows helps mitigate potential issues during integration, reducing the likelihood of disruptions to ongoing operations.

Customization Requirements: Financial institutions may have unique customization requirements based on their specific business processes or regulatory environments. While xVia offers a standardized API, it's essential to consider the flexibility and customization options available to accommodate these specific requirements. Collaborative efforts involve defining customization parameters to align with individual needs.

Security and Compliance: Ensuring the security of data transmitted through xVia's abstraction layer and compliance with regulatory standards are paramount considerations. Financial institutions and the developers of xVia collaborate to implement robust security measures, including encryption protocols and adherence to industry and regulatory standards. Proactive engagement with regulatory authorities ensures that the abstraction layer provided by xVia aligns with evolving compliance requirements.

Conclusion: Unifying Cross-Border Payments with xVia's Abstraction Layer:

xVia's abstraction layer over RippleNet emerges as a unifying force, simplifying the intricacies of cross-border payments for financial institutions. By providing a standardized interface, xVia abstracts complexities and offers financial institutions a seamless gateway to RippleNet. As we progress through subsequent chapters, we will continue to explore how xVia reshapes the landscape of cross-border payments, unlocking new possibilities for efficiency, adaptability, and innovation.

Easy Integration for Business Applications

In the ever-evolving landscape of cross-border payments, the seamless integration of payment solutions with diverse business applications is a key driver of efficiency and innovation. xVia, an integral component of Ripple's suite of solutions, plays a pivotal role as a standard API for payments, facilitating easy integration with various business applications. This chapter explores the transformative subtopic of "Easy Integration for Business Applications," delving into how xVia streamlines the integration process, enabling financial institutions to enhance their services and capabilities.

The Significance of Integration in Payments:

Before delving into the specifics of xVia's role in facilitating easy integration for business applications, it's essential to understand the broader significance of integration in the context of cross-border payments.

Integration as a Catalyst for Efficiency: Integration involves the seamless connection and interaction between different systems, allowing them to work together harmoniously. In the realm of cross-border payments, integration is a catalyst for operational efficiency, enabling financial institutions to streamline workflows, reduce manual intervention, and provide enhanced services to their customers.

Enabling Interconnected Services: The integration of payment solutions with various business applications fosters an ecosystem where financial services are interconnected with other facets of business operations. This interconnectedness empowers financial institutions to offer a broader range of services, respond more effectively to market demands, and create a cohesive user experience for their customers.

Empowering Financial Institutions with xVia's Integration Capabilities:

xVia's role as a standard API for payments extends beyond facilitating transactions—it serves as a bridge that enables the easy integration of payment solutions with a multitude of business applications. This section explores the key features and mechanisms through which xVia simplifies the integration process, fostering a seamless connection between cross-border payments and diverse business applications.

Unified Interface for Business Applications: At the core of xVia's integration capabilities is its provision of a unified interface for business applications. Financial institutions can connect to xVia through a standardized API, abstracting the complexities of cross-border payments and providing a simplified interface for integration with various business applications.

This unified interface ensures that financial institutions can seamlessly integrate xVia with their existing business applications, regardless of the technologies and platforms they use. The standardization of the integration process contributes to operational efficiency, reduces development efforts, and accelerates the implementation of new services.

Adaptability to Diverse Business Environments: Recognizing the diversity of business environments and applications used by financial institutions, xVia's integration capabilities are designed to be adaptable. Financial institutions can connect to xVia using their preferred programming languages, communication protocols, and technology stacks, ensuring compatibility with their unique business environments.

This adaptability is crucial for financial institutions with varied business applications, allowing them to leverage the benefits of cross-border payments without significant modifications to their existing business infrastructure. xVia's integration capabilities act as a versatile bridge that accommodates the specific requirements of each financial institution's business environment.

Reducing Development Complexity: Integration projects are often characterized by their complexity, requiring significant development efforts to ensure compatibility between different systems. xVia addresses this challenge by reducing the development complexity associated with integrating cross-border payments into business applications.

Financial institutions leveraging xVia benefit from a standardized API and data format for interactions with cross-border payment networks. This standardization streamlines the development process, eliminating the need for extensive customizations and reducing the time and resources required for integration projects.

Seamless Data Exchange: xVia ensures seamless data exchange between cross-border payment networks and business applications. Financial institutions can send payment instructions to xVia using a standardized data structure, and xVia takes care of translating and formatting the data according to the requirements of the cross-border payment network.

This seamless data exchange simplifies the integration process, allowing financial institutions to focus on enhancing their business applications rather than dealing with the intricacies of cross-border payment data formats. The result is a more streamlined and efficient integration experience.

Benefits of Easy Integration for Business Applications:

The easy integration facilitated by xVia between cross-border payments and business applications brings forth a range of benefits for financial institutions. This section explores these benefits and the positive impact on operational efficiency, innovation, and customer experience.

Operational Efficiency and Automation: Easy integration between cross-border payments and business applications enhances operational efficiency by reducing manual intervention and streamlining workflows. Financial institutions can automate key processes related to cross-border payments, such as reconciliation and reporting, seamlessly integrating these functions into their business applications.

The automation of processes contributes to operational excellence, allowing financial institutions to allocate resources strategically and focus on value-added activities. By leveraging xVia's easy integration capabilities, financial institutions achieve a more efficient and automated cross-border payment ecosystem.

Innovative Service Offerings: The easy integration facilitated by xVia opens the door to innovative service offerings for financial institutions. By seamlessly incorporating cross-border payments into various business applications, financial institutions can explore new ways to provide value to their customers.

For example, integrating cross-border payments with supply chain management systems can enable real-time payment settlements for international trade transactions. Similarly, integrating with e-commerce platforms can offer customers seamless and cost-effective cross-border payment options. xVia's easy integration capabilities empower financial institutions to innovate and differentiate their service offerings in a competitive market.

Enhanced Customer Experience: Integration between cross-border payments and business applications contributes to an enhanced customer experience. Financial institutions can provide their customers with a seamless and integrated payment journey, reducing friction and offering a more convenient and efficient cross-border payment experience.

For instance, integrating cross-border payments with mobile banking applications allows customers to initiate and track international transactions seamlessly. The unified interface provided by xVia ensures that customers experience a cohesive and user-friendly interaction, fostering satisfaction and loyalty.

Speed to Market for New Services: The easy integration capabilities of xVia accelerate the speed to market for new cross-border payment services. Financial institutions can swiftly implement and launch innovative services by leveraging xVia's standardized API and integration features.

Reduced development complexity and streamlined integration processes enable financial institutions to bring new services to market more rapidly. This agility is crucial in a fast-paced industry, allowing financial institutions to stay ahead of competition and capitalize on emerging market trends.

Real-World Examples of Integration Success:

Examining real-world examples provides tangible illustrations of how financial institutions have benefited from xVia's easy integration capabilities in their cross-border payment operations.

Integrating with ERP Systems at SBI Holdings: SBI Holdings, a financial services company in Japan, utilized xVia to seamlessly integrate cross-border payments with its Enterprise Resource Planning (ERP) systems. The standardized interface provided by xVia allowed SBI Holdings to streamline payment workflows, automate reconciliation processes, and enhance operational efficiency.

The integration with ERP systems enabled SBI Holdings to optimize its internal processes and provide a more integrated and efficient cross-border payment experience for its corporate clients. The success of SBI Holdings showcased the transformative impact of xVia's easy integration capabilities.

Empowering Mobile Banking at Standard Chartered: Standard Chartered, a global banking institution, leveraged xVia to integrate cross-border payments with its mobile banking applications. The unified interface provided by xVia enabled Standard Chartered to offer its customers a seamless and user-friendly experience for international transactions through mobile devices.

The integration with mobile banking applications enhanced the speed and convenience of cross-border payments, contributing to an improved customer experience. Standard Chartered's success demonstrated how xVia's easy integration capabilities empower financial institutions to innovate in the digital banking landscape.

Challenges and Considerations in Integration:

While xVia simplifies the integration process between cross-border payments and business applications, certain challenges and considerations should be addressed to ensure successful implementation and operation.

Data Mapping and Transformation: Mapping and transforming data between cross-border payment networks and business applications require careful consideration. Financial institutions and the developers of xVia collaborate to define and align data flows, ensuring accurate and seamless data exchange.

A comprehensive understanding of data mapping and transformation is essential to avoid data discrepancies and ensure that information is accurately transmitted between systems. Collaborative efforts during this phase contribute to the success of the integration project.

Security and Compliance: Ensuring the security of data transmitted between cross-border payment networks and business applications is a critical consideration. Financial institutions and the developers of xVia collaborate to implement robust security measures, including encryption protocols and adherence to industry and regulatory standards.

Proactive engagement with regulatory authorities ensures that the integration aligns with evolving compliance requirements. Security and compliance considerations are integral to building trust and safeguarding sensitive information in the cross-border payment ecosystem.

User Training and Adoption: The successful integration of cross-border payments with business applications requires user training and adoption strategies. Financial institutions should invest in educating their teams and end-users on the new functionalities introduced through integration, ensuring a smooth transition and maximizing the benefits of the integrated ecosystem.

User training and adoption efforts involve providing comprehensive documentation, conducting training sessions, and offering ongoing support to address any challenges or questions that may arise during the adoption phase.

Conclusion: Transformative Integration with xVia's Easy Integration Capabilities:

xVia's role as a standard API for payments extends beyond transaction facilitation—it serves as a catalyst for transformative integration between cross-border payments and business applications. By providing a unified interface and streamlining the integration process, xVia empowers financial institutions to enhance their operational efficiency, innovate their service offerings, and deliver a superior customer experience. As we progress through subsequent chapters, we will continue to explore how xVia reshapes the landscape of cross-border payments, unlocking new possibilities for integration, efficiency, and customer-centric solutions.

Reduces Need for Manual Reconciliation

In the intricate world of cross-border payments, manual reconciliation has long been a labor-intensive and error-prone process. Financial institutions grapple with the challenges of matching transactions, resolving discrepancies, and ensuring accuracy in the midst of diverse payment networks and systems. xVia, a pivotal component of Ripple's suite of solutions, emerges as a transformative force in mitigating these challenges. This chapter explores the impactful subtopic of "Reduces Need for Manual Reconciliation," delving into how xVia streamlines reconciliation processes, enhances accuracy, and elevates operational efficiency for financial institutions.

Understanding the Burden of Manual Reconciliation:

Before delving into the specifics of how xVia alleviates the need for manual reconciliation, it's essential to comprehend the burden that manual reconciliation imposes on financial institutions in the context of cross-border payments.

Complexities in Cross-Border Payment Reconciliation: Cross-border payments involve a myriad of payment networks, settlement systems, and financial institutions, each with its own set of protocols and data formats. As a result, reconciling transactions across these diverse systems becomes a complex task, requiring meticulous attention to detail and often leading to extended reconciliation cycles.

Challenges of Discrepancies and Errors: Manual reconciliation is prone to discrepancies and errors, stemming from differences in data formats, communication protocols, and processing times across various payment networks. Identifying and resolving these discrepancies is not only time-consuming but also poses the risk of financial inaccuracies and operational inefficiencies.

Operational Impact and Resource Allocation: The labor-intensive nature of manual reconciliation consumes valuable resources within financial institutions. Teams are tasked with the arduous process of matching transactions, investigating discrepancies, and ensuring compliance, diverting focus from strategic initiatives and customer-centric activities.

Empowering Financial Institutions with xVia's Reconciliation Capabilities:

xVia's role as a standard API for payments extends beyond transaction facilitation—it serves as a solution that significantly reduces the need for manual reconciliation. This section explores the key features and mechanisms through which xVia streamlines reconciliation processes, empowers financial institutions, and elevates operational efficiency.

Automated Transaction Data Standardization: At the core of xVia's reconciliation capabilities is its ability to automate the standardization of transaction data. When financial institutions initiate cross-border payments through xVia, the platform standardizes transaction data according to a unified format. This automated standardization ensures consistency in data across various payment networks and systems.

The standardized data format encompasses essential transaction details such as payment amount, currency, sender and receiver information, and timestamps. By automating this standardization process, xVia eliminates the need for manual intervention in aligning data formats, significantly reducing the likelihood of discrepancies during reconciliation.

Real-time Transaction Visibility: xVia provides real-time visibility into the status and progress of cross-border transactions. Financial institutions can monitor the lifecycle of transactions as they traverse through the interconnected networks. Real-time visibility empowers institutions with instant access to transaction details, settlement confirmations, and any potential issues that may arise.

This transparency ensures that financial institutions have up-to-the-minute information, reducing the time and effort required for manual reconciliation. It enables proactive identification and resolution of discrepancies, contributing to enhanced accuracy in financial reporting and compliance.

Instant Settlement Confirmation: In the traditional cross-border payment landscape, settlement confirmations often lag behind the initiation of transactions, leading to uncertainties and delays in reconciliation. xVia transforms this paradigm by providing instant settlement confirmations. As transactions are settled in real-time between endpoints, financial institutions receive immediate confirmation of successful settlement.

This instant settlement confirmation not only accelerates the overall payment process but also eliminates the need for prolonged reconciliation cycles. Financial institutions can rely on the timely and accurate information provided by xVia, reducing the operational burden associated with manual reconciliation efforts.

Data Enrichment and Contextual Information: xVia enhances transaction data by providing additional contextual information that aids in reconciliation. This includes details such as payment purpose, reference numbers, and relevant contextual information associated with each transaction. By enriching transaction data, xVia equips financial institutions with comprehensive information that facilitates quicker and more accurate reconciliation.

The availability of contextual information reduces the reliance on manual investigation to understand the nature and purpose of transactions. Financial institutions can leverage this enriched data to streamline reconciliation processes and allocate resources more strategically.

Benefits of Reducing Manual Reconciliation:

The reduction of manual reconciliation facilitated by xVia yields a range of benefits for financial institutions engaged in cross-border payments. This section explores these benefits and the positive impact on operational efficiency, accuracy, and resource allocation.

Operational Efficiency and Time Savings: One of the primary benefits of reducing manual reconciliation is the enhancement of operational efficiency and significant time savings. xVia's automated standardization of transaction data, real-time visibility, and instant settlement confirmations contribute to streamlined reconciliation processes.

Financial institutions no longer need to allocate extensive resources to manually match transactions or investigate discrepancies. The reduction in manual intervention accelerates the overall reconciliation cycle, enabling teams to focus on more value-added activities and strategic initiatives.

Enhanced Accuracy in Financial Reporting: The automated standardization of transaction data and real-time visibility provided by xVia contribute to enhanced accuracy in financial reporting. Financial institutions can rely on the standardized and up-to-date information available through xVia for reconciliation purposes.

Reducing the manual reconciliation burden minimizes the risk of errors and discrepancies, ensuring that financial reports reflect the most accurate and current state of cross-border transactions. This accuracy is crucial for compliance, audit processes, and maintaining the integrity of financial records.

Resource Allocation to Strategic Initiatives: By alleviating the need for extensive manual reconciliation efforts, financial institutions can redirect resources to more strategic initiatives. Teams that were previously engaged in labor-intensive reconciliation tasks can now contribute to activities that drive innovation, improve customer experiences, and support the institution's overall growth objectives.

The redirection of resources enhances the agility of financial institutions, allowing them to respond more effectively to market dynamics, explore new business opportunities, and stay ahead of industry trends.

Compliance Assurance: Reducing the manual reconciliation burden through xVia contributes to compliance assurance. The platform's automated standardization and real-time visibility features ensure that financial institutions have access to accurate and timely information, aligning with regulatory requirements.

The assurance of compliance reduces the risk of penalties or fines associated with inaccuracies in financial reporting. Financial institutions can demonstrate a commitment to adherence to regulatory standards, building trust with regulators and stakeholders.

Real-World Examples of Reconciliation Success:

Examining real-world examples provides tangible illustrations of how financial institutions have benefited from xVia's reconciliation capabilities in their cross-border payment operations.

Streamlining Reconciliation at HSBC: HSBC, a global banking institution, utilized xVia to streamline reconciliation processes across its cross-border payment operations. The automated standardization of transaction data and real-time visibility provided by xVia enabled HSBC to reduce the time and effort required for manual reconciliation.

The streamlined reconciliation processes at HSBC contributed to enhanced operational efficiency, allowing the institution to allocate resources strategically and focus on delivering superior services to its customers. HSBC's success demonstrated the transformative impact of xVia in reconciling cross-border transactions.

Improving Accuracy at BNP Paribas: BNP Paribas, a leading European bank, leveraged xVia to improve the accuracy of reconciliation in its cross-border payment workflows. The platform's instant settlement confirmations and data enrichment features provided BNP Paribas with comprehensive and up-to-date information for reconciliation.

The improved accuracy in reconciliation processes at BNP Paribas positively impacted financial reporting, compliance adherence, and overall operational efficiency. BNP Paribas showcased how xVia's reconciliation capabilities contribute to a more accurate and reliable cross-border payment ecosystem.

Challenges and Considerations in Reconciliation:

While xVia simplifies and reduces the need for manual reconciliation, certain challenges and considerations should be addressed to ensure successful implementation and operation.

Data Discrepancies and Disputes: Despite xVia's automated standardization, occasional data discrepancies and disputes may arise, especially when interfacing with diverse payment networks. Financial institutions and the developers of xVia collaborate to establish protocols for resolving discrepancies and handling disputes in a timely and efficient manner.

A proactive approach to addressing data discrepancies ensures that reconciliation processes remain smooth and that any issues are promptly identified and resolved.

Integration with Legacy Systems: Financial institutions often operate with legacy systems that may have limitations in adapting to automated reconciliation processes. Collaborative efforts between financial institutions and the developers of xVia involve addressing the integration challenges associated with legacy systems, ensuring seamless compatibility and data exchange.

Considerations for legacy system integration are crucial to maximizing the benefits of xVia's reconciliation capabilities across diverse technology environments.

Continuous Monitoring and Improvement: The dynamic nature of the cross-border payment landscape requires continuous monitoring and improvement of reconciliation processes. Financial institutions should establish mechanisms for ongoing monitoring of transaction data, reconciliation outcomes, and the overall performance of xVia.

Continuous improvement efforts involve staying abreast of updates in payment networks, addressing emerging challenges, and optimizing reconciliation processes to align with evolving industry standards.

Conclusion: Revolutionizing Cross-Border Payments with Reduced Manual Reconciliation

xVia emerges as a revolutionary solution in the realm of cross-border payments by significantly reducing the need for manual reconciliation. Through its automated standardization, real-time visibility, and instant settlement confirmations, xVia empowers financial institutions to streamline reconciliation processes, enhance accuracy, and allocate resources strategically.

As we progress through subsequent chapters, we will continue to explore how xVia reshapes the landscape of cross-border payments, unlocking new possibilities for operational efficiency, compliance assurance, and customer-centric solutions.

Chapter 5: Use Cases - RippleNet in the Real World
Santander Bank Implementation for Retail Customers

In the rapidly evolving landscape of cross-border payments, financial institutions are continually seeking innovative solutions to enhance the speed, cost-effectiveness, and efficiency of international transactions. Santander, a global banking giant, stands out as a pioneer in embracing RippleNet—a decentralized network powered by blockchain technology. This section explores the real-world use case of Santander's implementation of RippleNet, focusing specifically on its transformative impact on retail customers.

The Imperative for Innovation in Cross-Border Payments:

Cross-border payments have historically been plagued by inefficiencies, delays, and high costs. Traditional correspondent banking models often involve a series of intermediaries, leading to extended settlement times and increased transaction fees. In this context, financial institutions face the imperative to innovate and adopt solutions that address these longstanding challenges.

Santander's Commitment to Innovation: Santander, one of the world's largest and most forward-thinking banks, has been at the forefront of embracing technological advancements to improve its services. Recognizing the limitations of traditional cross-border payment systems, Santander sought a transformative solution to enhance the customer experience for its retail clients.

Enter RippleNet: Revolutionizing Cross-Border Payments

RippleNet, developed by Ripple, represents a paradigm shift in cross-border payments. Leveraging blockchain technology, RippleNet provides financial institutions with a decentralized and interoperable network that facilitates seamless, secure, and near-instantaneous cross-border transactions. Santander's implementation of RippleNet for its retail customers showcases the tangible benefits of this innovative solution.

The RippleNet Ecosystem: Before delving into Santander's implementation, it's essential to understand the foundational principles of the RippleNet ecosystem. RippleNet comprises a network of financial institutions, payment service providers, and banks that leverage blockchain technology to enable real-time, low-cost cross-border payments. The decentralized nature of RippleNet eliminates the need for intermediaries, reducing settlement times and transaction costs.

RippleNet operates through three primary solutions: xCurrent, xRapid, and xVia. xCurrent facilitates real-time, end-to-end tracking of payments. xRapid utilizes the digital asset XRP to provide on-demand liquidity, minimizing costs. xVia serves as a standard API for payments, simplifying the integration process for financial institutions.

Santander's RippleNet Implementation Journey:

Santander embarked on its journey with RippleNet to address the challenges inherent in cross-border payments. The bank's focus was on providing its retail customers with a superior and efficient international payment experience.

Enhancing Speed and Efficiency: One of the key motivations behind Santander's adoption of RippleNet was to enhance the speed and efficiency of cross-border transactions. Traditional methods often involve multiple correspondent banks, leading to delays in settlement. RippleNet's decentralized architecture enables direct and real-time transactions between participating financial institutions, significantly reducing settlement times.

For Santander's retail customers, this means a faster and more responsive international payment experience. Transactions that might have taken days to settle using traditional methods can now be completed in a matter of seconds, providing retail clients with unprecedented speed and convenience.

Cost Reduction and Transparent Fees: Cross-border transactions are notorious for their associated fees, including intermediary charges incurred along the payment journey. Santander recognized the opportunity to reduce these costs by leveraging RippleNet's xRapid solution, which utilizes the digital asset XRP to provide on-demand liquidity.

By utilizing XRP as a bridge currency, Santander minimizes the need for holding multiple fiat currencies in correspondent accounts, thus unlocking capital and reducing liquidity costs. This cost reduction is particularly impactful for retail customers, as it translates to more competitive and transparent fee structures for international transactions.

Seamless Integration and User-Friendly Experience: Santander's RippleNet implementation prioritized a seamless integration process and a user-friendly experience for its retail customers. xVia, Ripple's standard API for payments, played a crucial role in achieving this objective. The abstraction layer provided by xVia simplified the integration with RippleNet, allowing Santander to seamlessly connect with the decentralized network.

For retail customers, this translated into a more intuitive and user-friendly international payment experience. The complexities of cross-border transactions were abstracted away, allowing customers to initiate and track payments with ease through Santander's digital platforms.

Real-Time Tracking and Transparency: xCurrent, another component of RippleNet, empowers participants with real-time tracking and end-to-end transparency for cross-border payments. Santander's retail customers can now track the status of their international transactions in real-time, gaining visibility into each stage of the payment journey.

This transparency not only instills confidence in customers but also reduces the need for inquiries related to payment status.

Retail clients can enjoy a more informed and empowered experience, knowing the exact status and location of their funds throughout the transaction lifecycle.

Case Study: Santander's Retail Customer Experience

To illustrate the impact of Santander's RippleNet implementation on retail customers, let's delve into a hypothetical case study:

Scenario: Maria's International Payment

Maria, a Santander retail customer, needs to make an international payment to her family overseas. Traditionally, this process would involve complex correspondent banking networks, resulting in delays and unclear fees. However, with Santander's adoption of RippleNet, Maria's experience is transformed.

1. Initiation: Maria initiates the international payment through Santander's digital platform, specifying the recipient, amount, and purpose. The integration with RippleNet via xVia ensures a seamless initiation process, abstracting away the complexities of cross-border transactions.

2. Real-Time Tracking: As soon as the payment is initiated, Maria gains real-time visibility into the status of her transaction. The xCurrent solution within RippleNet enables Santander to provide Maria with end-to-end tracking, allowing her to monitor the progress of her payment in real-time.

3. On-Demand Liquidity with XRP: Santander utilizes xRapid, harnessing the benefits of XRP as a bridge currency to facilitate on-demand liquidity. This minimizes the need for holding multiple fiat currencies in correspondent accounts, reducing liquidity costs and offering Maria a more cost-effective international payment solution.

4. Near-Instant Settlement: Thanks to the decentralized nature of RippleNet, Maria's international payment settles near-instantaneously. The elimination of intermediaries and the direct

connection between Santander and the recipient's financial institution contribute to the speed and efficiency of settlement.

5. Transparent Fees: Maria benefits from transparent and competitive fees for her international payment. RippleNet's cost-effective solution, coupled with the use of XRP for liquidity, ensures that Maria receives a clear breakdown of fees associated with her transaction, promoting trust and transparency.

6. Confirmation and Notification: Upon successful settlement, Maria receives instant confirmation of her payment. Santander's digital platform notifies her of the completed transaction, providing peace of mind and assurance that her funds have reached the intended recipient.

Key Takeaways from Santander's RippleNet Implementation:

Santander's RippleNet implementation for retail customers showcases several key takeaways that highlight the transformative impact of blockchain-based solutions in cross-border payments:

Empowered Retail Customers: Retail customers like Maria experience a paradigm shift in their international payment journeys. The real-time tracking, transparency, and speed afforded by RippleNet empower customers, providing them with greater control and confidence in their cross-border transactions.

Cost-Effective Solutions: The use of RippleNet's xRapid solution and XRP as a bridge currency contributes to cost reduction for both Santander and its retail customers. By minimizing liquidity costs and offering transparent fees, Santander delivers a more cost-effective and competitive solution in the cross-border payments landscape.

Seamless Integration and User-Friendly Experience: Santander's prioritization of a seamless integration process, facilitated by xVia, results in a user-friendly experience for retail customers. The abstraction of complex technical details ensures that customers can initiate and track international payments with ease, even if they are not well-versed in blockchain technology.

Enhanced Trust and Transparency: RippleNet's decentralized architecture, real-time tracking, and transparent fees contribute to enhanced trust and transparency in cross-border payments. Retail customers can rely on Santander's adoption of RippleNet to provide a trustworthy and streamlined international payment experience.

Reduced Settlement Times: The elimination of intermediaries and the direct connection between financial institutions on RippleNet lead to near-instant settlement times. Retail customers benefit from reduced waiting periods, allowing them to experience faster and more responsive cross-border transactions.

Future Potential for Innovation: Santander's RippleNet implementation opens the door to future potential for innovation in cross-border payments. As blockchain technology continues to evolve, financial institutions can explore additional use cases and enhancements to further improve the customer experience.

Challenges and Considerations:

While Santander's implementation of RippleNet for retail customers presents a compelling success story, certain challenges and considerations should be acknowledged:

Regulatory Compliance: The adoption of blockchain technology in cross-border payments necessitates adherence to evolving regulatory frameworks. Financial institutions, including Santander, must navigate the complex landscape of international regulations to ensure compliance while leveraging innovative solutions.

Education and Awareness: The successful implementation of RippleNet requires educating retail customers about the benefits and functionalities of blockchain-based solutions. Financial institutions must invest in awareness campaigns and educational initiatives to ensure that customers understand the transformative nature of the adopted technology.

Network Effects and Adoption: The effectiveness of RippleNet in cross-border payments relies on widespread adoption across the financial industry. Santander's success is contingent on other financial institutions joining the network, creating a robust ecosystem that maximizes the benefits of blockchain technology.

Conclusion: Santander's RippleNet Implementation - Transforming Retail Cross-Border Payments

Santander's adoption of RippleNet for retail customers represents a significant leap forward in the evolution of cross-border payments. The bank's commitment to innovation, cost-effectiveness, and customer-centric solutions is exemplified by the transformative impact of RippleNet on the retail customer experience.

As we delve further into the diverse use cases of RippleNet in subsequent chapters, we will uncover additional success stories and explore the broader implications of blockchain technology in shaping the future of cross-border payments. The real-world implementation at Santander serves as a beacon of inspiration for financial institutions seeking to revolutionize their approach to international transactions and enhance the overall customer journey.

MoneyGram Using xRapid for Cheaper Remittances

In the realm of cross-border payments, the remittance industry stands as a crucial component, facilitating the flow of funds between individuals and families across borders. However, traditional remittance models have long been associated with high fees, delays, and inefficiencies. MoneyGram, a leading money transfer company, has emerged as an innovator in the space by harnessing Ripple's xRapid solution to revolutionize remittances. This section delves into the real-world use case of MoneyGram utilizing xRapid, focusing on how this adoption has led to cheaper and more efficient remittances.

Challenges in Traditional Remittance Models:

Before delving into the specifics of MoneyGram's use of xRapid, it's essential to understand the challenges that have historically plagued traditional remittance models.

High Transaction Costs: Traditional remittance methods often involve multiple intermediaries, each charging fees for their services. As funds traverse through the correspondent banking network, these fees accumulate, leading to high overall transaction costs for both senders and recipients.

Delays in Settlement: The multi-step process of traditional remittances introduces delays in settlement times. Funds may pass through several correspondent banks before reaching the intended recipient, resulting in extended waiting periods for individuals relying on timely remittances.

Lack of Transparency: Traditional remittance models can lack transparency, making it challenging for senders and recipients to track the status and location of funds in real-time. The opacity in the payment journey can lead to uncertainty and anxiety for those depending on remittances for essential needs.

Enter Ripple's xRapid: Transforming Remittances

Ripple's xRapid solution, part of the broader RippleNet ecosystem, addresses these challenges by leveraging the digital asset XRP as a bridge currency. The decentralized and real-time nature of xRapid facilitates on-demand liquidity, reducing costs and settlement times for cross-border payments. MoneyGram's adoption of xRapid exemplifies how innovative solutions can bring about positive change in the remittance industry.

MoneyGram's Pioneering Adoption of xRapid:

MoneyGram, a global money transfer company with a vast network spanning over 200 countries and territories, recognized the need for innovation in the remittance space. In 2018, MoneyGram entered into a strategic partnership with Ripple, aiming to explore the transformative potential of blockchain technology, particularly xRapid.

Key Components of MoneyGram's xRapid Implementation:

Utilizing XRP as a Bridge Currency: One of the key features of xRapid is its utilization of XRP as a bridge currency. In the traditional correspondent banking model, financial institutions hold various fiat currencies in correspondent accounts to facilitate cross-border payments. xRapid streamlines this process by utilizing XRP as a bridge currency, minimizing the need for maintaining multiple fiat accounts.

On-Demand Liquidity: xRapid provides on-demand liquidity by converting the sender's currency into XRP, transmitting it across borders, and converting it back into the recipient's currency at the destination. This process occurs in real-time, enabling near-instantaneous settlement and reducing the dependency on pre-funded accounts.

Cost Reduction through XRP: The use of XRP as a bridge currency introduces cost efficiencies in the remittance process. By minimizing the need for holding pre-funded accounts in multiple currencies, xRapid reduces liquidity costs for financial institutions and money transfer companies like MoneyGram. These cost savings can be passed on to customers, resulting in cheaper remittance options.

Enhanced Speed and Transparency: The decentralized nature of xRapid, coupled with the speed of XRP transactions, significantly enhances the speed of remittances. Transactions settle in a matter of seconds, providing a more responsive experience for both senders and recipients. Additionally, the transparency of the XRP ledger allows for real-time tracking and visibility into the payment journey.

Impact on Remittance Costs and Affordability:

MoneyGram's adoption of xRapid has had a profound impact on the cost dynamics of remittances, making international money transfers more affordable for individuals and families.

Reduction in Transaction Fees: Traditional remittance models often involve a series of fees incurred at each stage of the payment journey. With xRapid, the use of XRP as a bridge currency streamlines the process, reducing the number of intermediaries and associated fees. MoneyGram can pass on these cost savings to customers, resulting in a noticeable reduction in transaction fees.

Competitive Pricing for Customers: MoneyGram's adoption of xRapid allows the company to offer more competitive pricing for remittances. Lower transaction fees and reduced overall costs make international money transfers a more attractive and affordable option for customers, especially those who depend on remittances for their daily needs.

Improving Remittance Accessibility: By lowering transaction costs, MoneyGram's use of xRapid enhances the accessibility of remittance services. Individuals who may have been deterred by high fees in the past are now presented with a more cost-effective solution, fostering financial inclusion and ensuring that remittance services are accessible to a broader population.

Real-World Impact: Case Studies and Examples:

Examining real-world examples provides tangible illustrations of how MoneyGram's adoption of xRapid has impacted remittance processes and affordability.

Case Study: Maria's Monthly Remittance

Maria, an expatriate worker living in the United States, sends a monthly remittance to her family in Mexico to support their living expenses. Before MoneyGram's adoption of xRapid, Maria experienced significant challenges:

1. High Fees: Maria incurred substantial fees at both ends of the remittance journey. The traditional correspondent banking model involved fees charged by the sending bank, intermediary banks, and the receiving bank in Mexico.

2. Long Waiting Periods: The multi-step process led to extended settlement times, and it often took several days for the funds to reach her family in Mexico.

3. Uncertainty in Exchange Rates: Fluctuations in exchange rates between the U.S. dollar and the Mexican peso led to uncertainty regarding the final amount her family would receive.

Post-Implementation with xRapid:

1. Reduced Transaction Fees: MoneyGram's adoption of xRapid significantly reduced the overall transaction fees associated with Maria's remittance. The streamlined process and the use of XRP as a bridge currency minimized intermediary charges, resulting in cost savings.

2. Near-Instant Settlement: With xRapid, Maria's monthly remittance settled near-instantaneously. The on-demand liquidity provided by XRP eliminated the delays associated with the traditional model, ensuring that her family received the funds promptly.

3. Transparent and Competitive Exchange Rates: MoneyGram's integration with xRapid brought transparency to

exchange rates. Maria could view real-time rates on the XRP ledger, providing clarity on the amount her family would receive in Mexican pesos. The competitive pricing made the remittance process more predictable and reliable.

Challenges and Considerations:

While MoneyGram's adoption of xRapid has brought about significant improvements, certain challenges and considerations should be acknowledged:

Market Volatility and XRP Price Fluctuations: The value of XRP, like other digital assets, can experience volatility. Fluctuations in XRP prices may impact the overall cost dynamics of remittances. MoneyGram and users need to consider strategies to mitigate the impact of market volatility on the affordability of remittance services.

Regulatory Compliance and Adoption: The regulatory landscape surrounding digital assets and blockchain technology continues to evolve. MoneyGram's success with xRapid is contingent on navigating regulatory frameworks across various jurisdictions. Additionally, broader industry adoption is essential for maximizing the benefits of xRapid.

Educating Users and Building Trust: The transition from traditional remittance models to blockchain-based solutions requires educating users about the advantages and functionalities of xRapid. Building trust in the security and reliability of digital assets is crucial for widespread adoption.

Conclusion: MoneyGram's xRapid Adoption - A Catalyst for Affordable Remittances

MoneyGram's strategic adoption of xRapid represents a pivotal moment in the evolution of the remittance industry. By leveraging the speed, efficiency, and cost-effectiveness of xRapid, MoneyGram has not only transformed its own operations but has also played a role in making international remittances more affordable for individuals and families worldwide.

As we explore additional use cases in the subsequent sections, we will uncover the broader implications of blockchain-based solutions in reshaping the landscape of cross-border payments and remittances. MoneyGram's journey with xRapid serves as a compelling example of how innovation in financial technology can create tangible and positive impacts on the lives of individuals relying on remittances for their financial well-being.

MercuryFX: Transferring Payments in Minutes

In the dynamic landscape of cross-border payments, the need for faster, more efficient, and cost-effective solutions is paramount. MercuryFX, a global currency specialist, has emerged as a frontrunner in leveraging RippleNet to revolutionize the speed and reliability of international payments. This section explores the real-world use case of MercuryFX, focusing on how the company's adoption of RippleNet enables the transfer of payments in a matter of minutes.

Challenges in Traditional Cross-Border Payments:

Traditional cross-border payment systems have long grappled with challenges that hinder the seamless flow of funds between countries.

Protracted Settlement Times: The traditional correspondent banking model involves a series of intermediaries through which funds must pass before reaching the recipient. This multi-step process contributes to protracted settlement times, with transactions often taking days to complete.

Inefficiencies and High Costs: Intermediaries and the reliance on pre-funded accounts in multiple currencies introduce inefficiencies and contribute to high transaction costs. The need to maintain liquidity across various accounts ties up capital and amplifies the overall expense of cross-border transactions.

Lack of Real-Time Visibility: Traditional systems lack real-time visibility into the status and location of funds during the payment journey. This opacity can lead to uncertainty for both senders and recipients, as they are left in the dark about the progress of their transactions.

Enter MercuryFX and RippleNet: A Paradigm Shift in Payments

MercuryFX's adoption of RippleNet, a decentralized network powered by blockchain technology, represents a paradigm shift in the realm of cross-border payments. RippleNet's suite of solutions, including xCurrent, xRapid, and xVia, provides the tools necessary to address the shortcomings of traditional systems and deliver faster, more cost-effective, and transparent international payments.

MercuryFX's Journey with RippleNet:

MercuryFX, as a global currency specialist with a focus on delivering tailored currency solutions, recognized the need to modernize its cross-border payment infrastructure. In 2018, the company entered into a strategic partnership with Ripple, marking the beginning of a transformative journey.

Key Components of MercuryFX's RippleNet Implementation:

Real-Time Settlement with xCurrent: MercuryFX harnessed the power of xCurrent, a RippleNet solution that facilitates real-time, end-to-end tracking of payments. xCurrent's messaging protocol enables participants to communicate and settle transactions in real-time, eliminating the delays associated with traditional correspondent banking models.

On-Demand Liquidity with xRapid: To further enhance the efficiency of cross-border transactions, MercuryFX integrated xRapid into its operations. xRapid utilizes the digital asset XRP as a bridge currency, providing on-demand liquidity and minimizing the need for pre-funded accounts. This approach significantly reduces liquidity costs and accelerates settlement times.

Seamless Integration with xVia: To streamline the connectivity with other participants on RippleNet, MercuryFX adopted xVia, Ripple's standard API for payments. xVia serves as an abstraction layer, simplifying the integration process and enabling MercuryFX to connect seamlessly with various financial institutions and payment providers globally.

The MercuryFX RippleNet Experience:

Real-Time Payment Settlement: One of the primary advantages MercuryFX gained through its adoption of xCurrent is the ability to settle payments in real-time. The traditional model's reliance on batch processing and delayed settlement is replaced by instantaneous transaction settlement, providing a superior experience for both MercuryFX and its clients.

Real-time settlement is particularly impactful for businesses and individuals requiring swift access to funds. For example, companies engaged in international trade can benefit from the rapid settlement of invoices, ensuring timely payment and maintaining healthy cash flow.

On-Demand Liquidity and Faster Payments: MercuryFX's integration of xRapid into its cross-border payment workflow introduces the concept of on-demand liquidity. By utilizing XRP as a bridge currency, MercuryFX can source liquidity in real-time without the need to pre-fund accounts in multiple currencies.

The result is faster and more cost-effective payments. MercuryFX can offer its clients the ability to transfer funds internationally with minimal delays, enabling businesses to operate more efficiently and individuals to access their money promptly.

Competitive Advantage through Cost Efficiency: Reducing transaction costs is a key aspect of MercuryFX's RippleNet adoption. The elimination of intermediary banks and the need for pre-funded accounts contribute to significant cost savings. MercuryFX can pass these savings on to its clients, providing them with a more cost-effective alternative for cross-border payments.

The competitive advantage gained through cost efficiency enhances MercuryFX's position in the market. Clients seeking affordable and expedited international payment solutions are drawn to MercuryFX's services, contributing to the company's growth and market differentiation.

Enhanced Visibility and Transparency: xCurrent's messaging protocol provides MercuryFX and its clients with enhanced visibility into the payment journey. Participants can track transactions in real-time, gaining insights into each stage of the process. This transparency reduces uncertainty and enhances trust in the cross-border payment experience.

Clients of MercuryFX, whether businesses or individuals, appreciate the ability to monitor the status of their payments throughout the entire lifecycle. The real-time tracking feature is especially valuable for businesses managing multiple international transactions and requiring accurate and up-to-date information.

Case Study: Maria's Business Expansion

Maria, a small business owner based in the United Kingdom, decides to expand her e-commerce business into new international markets. Her success relies on the ability to receive timely payments from customers worldwide and efficiently manage cross-border transactions. Before MercuryFX's adoption of RippleNet:

1. Challenges with Delays: Maria faced delays in receiving payments from international customers due to the protracted settlement times of traditional payment methods. This delayed her ability to fulfill orders promptly.

2. High Transaction Costs: The high transaction costs associated with intermediary banks and currency conversion ate into Maria's profit margins, making it challenging to offer competitive pricing for her products.

3. Uncertainty in Payment Status: The lack of real-time visibility into payment status created uncertainty for Maria, impacting her ability to manage inventory and plan business operations effectively.

Post-Implementation with RippleNet:

1. Real-Time Settlement: MercuryFX's integration of xCurrent enables Maria to experience real-time settlement of international payments. As soon as a customer makes a purchase, Maria can see the funds settled in her account almost instantly, allowing her to fulfill orders promptly.

2. Cost-Efficient Transactions: With the adoption of xRapid, MercuryFX significantly reduces the transaction costs associated with Maria's international payments. The use of XRP as a bridge currency minimizes intermediary fees and currency conversion costs, ensuring that Maria retains a higher percentage of her earnings.

3. Visibility and Control: The enhanced visibility provided by xCurrent allows Maria to track the status of each transaction in real-time. She can monitor incoming payments, identify completed transactions, and plan her business operations with confidence, knowing the exact financial status of her e-commerce venture.

Challenges and Considerations:

While MercuryFX's adoption of RippleNet introduces substantial benefits, certain challenges and considerations should be acknowledged:

Regulatory Compliance: The cross-border payments industry operates within a complex regulatory landscape. MercuryFX must navigate and comply with varying regulatory requirements across different jurisdictions to ensure the seamless operation of its services.

Market Adoption and Ecosystem Growth: The success of RippleNet relies on widespread adoption and the growth of a robust ecosystem. MercuryFX's effectiveness in providing seamless cross-border payment solutions is contingent on the continued expansion of RippleNet's network and the participation of additional financial institutions and payment providers.

Education and Awareness: The transition from traditional payment methods to blockchain-based solutions requires educating businesses and individuals about the advantages and functionalities of RippleNet. MercuryFX must play a role in building awareness and fostering understanding among its client base.

Conclusion: MercuryFX's RippleNet Integration - Transforming Cross-Border Payments

MercuryFX's strategic integration of RippleNet represents a transformative leap forward in the realm of cross-border payments. The combination of xCurrent, xRapid, and xVia equips MercuryFX with the tools necessary to provide its clients with faster, more cost-effective, and transparent international payment solutions.

As we explore additional use cases in the subsequent sections, we will unveil the broader impact of RippleNet on diverse industries and examine how the adoption of blockchain-based solutions is reshaping the landscape of global payments. MercuryFX's journey serves as a compelling testament to the potential of innovative technologies to drive positive change and efficiency in the cross-border payments ecosystem.

Cuallix: Opening New Markets with XRP

In the ever-evolving landscape of cross-border payments, financial institutions are constantly seeking innovative solutions to expand their reach and open new markets. Cuallix, a forward-thinking financial services provider, has emerged as a pioneer in leveraging RippleNet and XRP to break barriers and reach untapped markets. This section explores the real-world use case of Cuallix, shedding light on how the adoption of RippleNet and XRP has empowered the company to open new markets and redefine its approach to international transactions.

Challenges in Expanding into New Markets:

Expanding into new markets presents financial institutions with a myriad of challenges, particularly in the realm of cross-border payments.

Limited Access to Banking Infrastructure: In many regions, especially in developing economies, the traditional banking infrastructure may be limited or inaccessible. This poses a significant hurdle for financial institutions looking to provide their services to populations in these areas.

High Transaction Costs and Inefficiencies: Entering new markets often involves navigating complex financial ecosystems with high transaction costs. Traditional correspondent banking models, with multiple intermediaries and pre-funded accounts, can amplify these costs and introduce inefficiencies.

Currency Exchange Challenges: Dealing with multiple currencies in diverse markets introduces complexities related to currency exchange. Fluctuating exchange rates and the need for various fiat accounts can make cross-border transactions intricate and expensive.

Cuallix's Strategic Approach with RippleNet and XRP:

Cuallix, as a financial services provider committed to innovation, recognized the need for a strategic approach to overcome the challenges associated with expanding into new markets. In 2017, the company embraced RippleNet and XRP, paving the way for a transformative journey.

Key Components of Cuallix's RippleNet and XRP Integration:

Efficient Cross-Border Payments with xRapid: Cuallix integrated xRapid into its cross-border payment infrastructure, harnessing the efficiency of XRP as a bridge currency. xRapid allows Cuallix to source liquidity in real-time, minimizing the need for pre-funded accounts in multiple currencies. This streamlined approach significantly reduces transaction costs and accelerates settlement times.

Rapid Integration with xVia: To facilitate seamless connectivity with diverse payment providers and financial institutions, Cuallix adopted xVia, Ripple's standard API for payments. xVia serves as an abstraction layer, simplifying the integration process and enabling Cuallix to connect with various entities globally.

Enhanced Visibility with xCurrent: Cuallix leveraged xCurrent to enhance the visibility and transparency of its cross-border transactions. The messaging protocol of xCurrent enables real-time tracking and end-to-end visibility, allowing Cuallix and its clients to monitor transactions throughout the payment journey.

The Cuallix RippleNet and XRP Experience:

Overcoming Banking Infrastructure Limitations: One of the primary advantages Cuallix gained through its RippleNet adoption was the ability to overcome limitations in banking infrastructure. In regions where traditional banking services were scarce, Cuallix could extend its reach and provide financial services to populations that were previously underserved.

By leveraging the decentralized nature of RippleNet and XRP, Cuallix created a more inclusive financial ecosystem. Individuals and businesses in areas with limited banking infrastructure could now access efficient cross-border payment solutions, fostering financial inclusion.

Reducing Transaction Costs and Improving Affordability: The integration of xRapid into Cuallix's payment workflow brought about a significant reduction in transaction costs. The use of XRP as a bridge currency streamlined the payment process, eliminating the need for maintaining pre-funded accounts in various currencies. As a result, Cuallix could offer more affordable cross-border payment solutions to its clients.

The affordability of transactions is particularly impactful in markets where individuals and businesses are sensitive to high fees. Cuallix's ability to provide cost-effective solutions positions the company as a preferred choice for those seeking accessible and affordable cross-border payments.

Navigating Currency Exchange Challenges: Cuallix's use of XRP as a bridge currency has proven instrumental in navigating the challenges associated with currency exchanges. The decentralized and borderless nature of XRP facilitates seamless currency conversion, allowing Cuallix to offer a unified solution for transactions involving different fiat currencies.

By leveraging XRP's ability to bridge various currencies, Cuallix provides clients with a simplified and cost-efficient method of conducting cross-border transactions. This approach minimizes the complexities associated with fluctuating exchange rates and reduces the reliance on maintaining accounts in multiple fiat currencies.

Case Study: Cuallix's Entry into the Latin American Market

Cuallix's strategic adoption of RippleNet and XRP played a pivotal role in the company's entry into the Latin American market, a region characterized by diverse currencies, limited banking infrastructure, and unique financial challenges.

1. Challenges in the Latin American Market:

- Limited access to traditional banking services for a significant portion of the population.
- High transaction costs associated with cross-border payments, hindering financial inclusivity.
- Currency exchange challenges in a region with multiple national currencies.

2. Cuallix's RippleNet and XRP Solution:
- Integration of xRapid for efficient cross-border payments, leveraging XRP as a bridge currency.
- Utilization of xVia for seamless integration with diverse payment providers in the Latin American market.
- Implementation of xCurrent for enhanced visibility and transparency in transactions.

3. Results and Impact:
- Cuallix successfully extended its services to previously underserved populations in Latin America.
- Transaction costs were significantly reduced, making cross-border payments more affordable for individuals and businesses.
- The decentralized and real-time nature of RippleNet empowered clients with transparent and efficient payment solutions.

Challenges and Considerations:

While Cuallix's RippleNet and XRP integration have brought about substantial benefits, certain challenges and considerations should be acknowledged:

Regulatory Compliance: Operating in diverse markets requires Cuallix to navigate and comply with varying regulatory frameworks. Adherence to local regulations and international standards is crucial for the seamless operation of cross-border payment services.

Educating Users and Building Trust: The introduction of innovative technologies such as RippleNet and XRP necessitates educating users about the advantages and functionalities of these solutions. Cuallix must play a role in building awareness and trust among its client base, ensuring a smooth transition to blockchain-based cross-border payments.

Market Adoption and Ecosystem Growth: The success of RippleNet relies on widespread adoption and the growth of a robust ecosystem. Cuallix's effectiveness in opening new markets is contingent on the continued expansion of RippleNet's network and the participation of additional financial institutions and payment providers.

Conclusion: Cuallix's RippleNet and XRP Integration - Redefining Cross-Border Payments

Cuallix's strategic adoption of RippleNet and XRP marks a significant milestone in the evolution of cross-border payments. By overcoming challenges associated with banking infrastructure, transaction costs, and currency exchanges, Cuallix has positioned itself as a catalyst for financial inclusion and market expansion.

As we explore additional use cases in the subsequent sections, we will uncover the broader impact of RippleNet on diverse industries and examine how the adoption of blockchain-based solutions is reshaping the landscape of global payments. Cuallix's journey serves as a compelling example of how innovative technologies can empower financial institutions to break barriers, reach new markets, and redefine the future of cross-border transactions.

Chapter 6: Beyond Payments - Smart Contracts and NFTs
Ability to Represent Any Asset on Ledger

In the ever-expanding landscape of blockchain technology, Ripple's ecosystem, particularly through the utilization of XRP and the XRP Ledger, transcends its original focus on cross-border payments. The ability to represent any asset on the ledger opens the door to a myriad of possibilities, revolutionizing how we perceive and interact with assets in the digital realm. This section delves into the profound implications of Ripple's XRP Ledger and its role in representing a diverse array of assets on the blockchain.

The Evolution of Asset Representation:

Traditionally, ledgers were confined to recording financial transactions, often limited to currencies and securities. However, the advent of blockchain technology, and particularly the XRP Ledger, has shattered these constraints. Ripple's vision extends beyond the scope of payments, embracing the notion that the ledger can serve as a decentralized and transparent repository for representing any form of value.

The XRP Ledger as a Decentralized Exchange:

At the core of this revolutionary capability is the decentralized exchange functionality embedded within the XRP Ledger. Unlike conventional exchanges that rely on centralized entities to facilitate trades, the XRP Ledger empowers users to exchange assets directly on the blockchain.

This decentralized exchange model opens up a world of possibilities, enabling users to trade and transfer various assets seamlessly. Whether it's fiat currencies, cryptocurrencies, commodities, or even digital representations of real-world assets, the XRP Ledger provides a decentralized platform for these transactions to occur.

Tokenization of Real-World Assets:

The ability to represent any asset on the ledger is exemplified through the process of tokenization. Tokenization involves creating digital tokens on the blockchain that are pegged to real-world assets. These tokens can then be traded, transferred, and owned on the blockchain, providing a digital representation of the underlying asset.

Real Estate Tokenization: One of the notable applications of representing assets on the XRP Ledger is the tokenization of real estate. Traditionally, real estate transactions are cumbersome, involving numerous intermediaries and paperwork. The XRP Ledger allows for the creation of digital tokens that represent ownership or shares in real estate properties.

Investors can purchase and trade these tokens on the decentralized exchange, enabling fractional ownership of real estate assets. This democratization of real estate investment not only enhances liquidity but also opens up investment opportunities to a broader range of individuals.

Tokenized Securities: In the realm of finance, traditional securities, such as stocks and bonds, are being transformed through tokenization. By representing these securities as digital tokens on the XRP Ledger, the cumbersome processes associated with traditional securities trading are streamlined.

Tokenized securities can be traded 24/7, and ownership transfers can occur almost instantaneously. This not only reduces friction in the financial markets but also introduces a new level of accessibility for a global audience of investors.

Digital Representations of Art and Collectibles: The XRP Ledger's ability to represent any asset extends to the world of art and collectibles. Physical assets like artwork can be tokenized, creating digital representations that are securely recorded on the blockchain. This introduces new possibilities for artists, collectors, and enthusiasts alike.

The transparent and immutable nature of the blockchain ensures provenance and authenticity, addressing challenges in the art market such as forgery and fraud. Digital representations of art can be traded globally, providing artists with new revenue streams and collectors with increased liquidity.

Enabling Cross-Border Asset Transfer:

The representation of any asset on the XRP Ledger not only transforms how we perceive ownership and trade but also revolutionizes cross-border asset transfers.

Seamless Cross-Border Transactions: Traditionally, transferring ownership of physical assets or securities across borders involved complex legal processes and intermediaries. The XRP Ledger's decentralized exchange and tokenization capabilities simplify this process.

Assets represented as tokens on the blockchain can be transferred seamlessly across borders. This not only reduces the time and costs associated with cross-border transactions but also eliminates the need for multiple intermediaries, enhancing the efficiency of global asset transfers.

Enhanced Liquidity and Accessibility: By representing any asset on the ledger, Ripple's ecosystem fosters enhanced liquidity and accessibility. Digital representations of assets can be traded globally, breaking down barriers and providing individuals with the ability to invest in a diverse range of assets.

This democratization of asset ownership is particularly impactful for regions with limited access to traditional financial systems. The XRP Ledger's decentralized nature ensures that individuals from around the world can participate in global markets without the need for traditional banking infrastructure.

Smart Contracts and Programmable Assets:

The representation of any asset on the XRP Ledger is further augmented by the integration of smart contracts. Smart contracts are self-executing contracts with the terms of the agreement directly written into code. Ripple's approach to smart contracts introduces programmable assets, enabling a new level of functionality and automation.

Programmable Assets: In the context of the XRP Ledger, programmable assets refer to digital tokens with embedded smart contract functionalities. These programmable assets can represent not only static assets but also dynamic conditions and rules.

For example, a tokenized asset on the XRP Ledger can be programmed to automatically distribute dividends to token holders based on predefined criteria. This level of automation introduces efficiency and transparency into traditional financial processes.

Decentralized Finance (DeFi) Applications: The combination of representing any asset on the ledger and smart contracts opens the door to a wide array of decentralized finance (DeFi) applications. Users can engage in lending, borrowing, and yield farming directly on the XRP Ledger, without the need for traditional financial intermediaries.

The decentralized and trustless nature of these applications aligns with the principles of blockchain technology, providing users with greater control over their financial assets. This decentralized approach to finance has the potential to reshape the traditional banking landscape.

Challenges and Considerations:

While the ability to represent any asset on the ledger introduces groundbreaking possibilities, certain challenges and considerations must be addressed:

Regulatory Compliance: Tokenization of assets and the introduction of programmable assets raise regulatory considerations. Ensuring compliance with diverse regulatory frameworks across jurisdictions is crucial for the widespread adoption of these innovations.

Security and Custody: As the value and complexity of tokenized assets increase, security and custody become paramount. Implementing robust security measures and establishing reliable custodial solutions are essential to safeguarding digital assets on the XRP Ledger.

Interoperability with Traditional Systems: For these innovations to achieve mainstream adoption, interoperability with traditional financial systems is vital. Bridging the gap between blockchain-based assets and legacy financial infrastructure requires collaboration and standardization.

Conclusion: The Transformative Power of Asset Representation on the XRP Ledger

Ripple's XRP Ledger, with its ability to represent any asset, stands at the forefront of a transformative shift in how we perceive, trade, and transfer value. The integration of tokenization and smart contracts expands the possibilities beyond traditional payments, ushering in a new era of decentralized finance and asset ownership.

As we explore additional facets of Ripple's ecosystem in the following sections, we will uncover the broader implications of these innovations on various industries. The XRP Ledger's role in representing any asset serves as a testament to the potential of blockchain technology to reshape the fundamental structures of our financial systems and unlock new opportunities for individuals and businesses worldwide.

Issuing, Trading, and Redeeming Tokenized Assets

In the dynamic landscape of blockchain technology, Ripple's XRP Ledger emerges as a pioneer in facilitating the issuance, trading, and redemption of tokenized assets. This transformative capability transcends the traditional boundaries of finance, opening up new avenues for individuals and businesses to interact with assets in the digital realm. This section explores the profound implications of Ripple's approach to tokenized assets, shedding light on how the XRP Ledger is reshaping the way we issue, trade, and redeem a diverse array of digital representations.

Tokenization on the XRP Ledger:

Tokenization is a fundamental concept that involves representing real-world assets as digital tokens on a blockchain. Ripple's XRP Ledger takes this concept to new heights by providing a decentralized and efficient platform for issuing, trading, and redeeming tokenized assets.

Issuing Tokenized Assets:

Unlocking New Possibilities for Asset Representation: The process of issuing tokenized assets on the XRP Ledger involves creating digital representations of physical or financial assets. These digital tokens are programmable and can represent a wide range of assets, including real estate, securities, commodities, and even unique digital assets like art.

By issuing tokenized assets on the XRP Ledger, individuals and businesses can unlock new possibilities for how they conceptualize and interact with assets. Each token is securely recorded on the blockchain, ensuring transparency, immutability, and traceability.

The Programmability Advantage: One of the distinguishing features of tokenized assets on the XRP Ledger is the programmability embedded in these tokens. Through smart contracts, token issuers can define specific conditions, rules, and functionalities associated with each token.

For instance, a real estate token can be programmed to automatically distribute rental income to token holders on a predetermined schedule. This level of automation introduces efficiency and transparency into the management of tokenized assets, transforming traditional financial processes.

Trading Tokenized Assets:

Decentralized Exchange Functionality: The XRP Ledger's decentralized exchange functionality plays a pivotal role in the seamless trading of tokenized assets. Unlike traditional exchanges that rely on centralized intermediaries to facilitate trades, the XRP Ledger allows users to trade tokens directly on the blockchain.

This decentralized exchange model introduces a new paradigm for asset trading, eliminating the need for multiple intermediaries and enabling peer-to-peer transactions. Users can buy, sell, and exchange tokenized assets in a trustless and transparent environment.

Enhanced Liquidity and Accessibility: The ability to trade tokenized assets on the XRP Ledger fosters enhanced liquidity and accessibility. Digital representations of assets can be traded 24/7, providing users with greater flexibility and responsiveness to market dynamics.

This enhanced liquidity is particularly impactful for traditionally illiquid assets, such as real estate or certain securities. Investors can now access a global marketplace for tokenized assets, contributing to a more efficient and inclusive financial ecosystem.

Fractional Ownership Opportunities: Tokenization on the XRP Ledger introduces the concept of fractional ownership, allowing investors to purchase and trade fractions of tokenized assets. This democratization of ownership enables a broader range of individuals to participate in the market, even with limited capital.

For example, an investor can own a fraction of a high-value real estate property by holding tokens representing a share in that property. This fractional ownership model enhances market participation and provides new investment opportunities.

Redeeming Tokenized Assets:

Efficient and Transparent Redemption: Redeeming tokenized assets on the XRP Ledger is a straightforward and efficient process. When an asset token represents ownership or entitlement to a specific real-world asset, redemption can be initiated by presenting the token to the issuing entity.

The redemption process is executed through the smart contract functionalities associated with the token. Smart contracts can automate the verification and redemption process, ensuring that it aligns with the predefined conditions set by the token issuer.

Unlocking Liquidity for Illiquid Assets: Tokenized assets on the XRP Ledger can unlock liquidity for traditionally illiquid assets. Investors holding tokens representing ownership in real estate, for example, can redeem their tokens and gain access to the underlying asset's value without the need for a lengthy and complex selling process.

This liquidity unlocking mechanism transforms how investors perceive and engage with traditionally illiquid assets. It provides an avenue for individuals to convert their digital assets back into tangible value when needed.

Case Study: Real Estate Tokenization and Redemption: Sarah, an investor based in a metropolitan area, decides to invest in real estate through tokenization on the XRP Ledger. She purchases tokens representing ownership in a commercial property. The tokens are programmed with smart contracts that define conditions for redemption.

Several months later, Sarah decides to redeem her tokens to access liquidity for a new investment opportunity. The redemption process is initiated by submitting her tokens to the issuing entity. The smart contracts associated with the tokens automatically verify the conditions for redemption.

Upon successful verification, Sarah receives the equivalent value in fiat currency or another agreed-upon form. The process is efficient, transparent, and provides Sarah with the liquidity she needs while maintaining the integrity and security of the tokenized asset.

Challenges and Considerations:

While the issuance, trading, and redemption of tokenized assets on the XRP Ledger introduce transformative possibilities, certain challenges and considerations must be addressed:

Regulatory Compliance: The tokenization of assets raises regulatory considerations, particularly regarding securities laws and ownership rights. Ensuring compliance with diverse regulatory frameworks across jurisdictions is crucial for the widespread adoption of tokenized assets.

Security and Custody: As the value and complexity of tokenized assets increase, security and custody become paramount. Implementing robust security measures and establishing reliable custodial solutions are essential to safeguarding digital assets on the XRP Ledger.

Interoperability with Traditional Systems: For these innovations to achieve mainstream adoption, interoperability with traditional financial systems is vital. Bridging the gap between blockchain-based assets and legacy financial infrastructure requires collaboration and standardization.

Conclusion: Transforming Asset Interactions with Tokenization on the XRP Ledger

Ripple's XRP Ledger, with its ability to facilitate the issuance, trading, and redemption of tokenized assets, stands at the forefront of a transformative shift in how individuals and businesses interact with value. The integration of tokenization on a decentralized platform introduces efficiency, transparency, and accessibility to the world of asset representation.

As we explore additional facets of Ripple's ecosystem in the following sections, we will uncover the broader implications of these innovations on various industries. The XRP Ledger's role in tokenizing assets represents a paradigm shift in how we perceive, trade, and redeem value, unlocking new opportunities for financial inclusion and redefining the landscape of digital finance.

Programmable Swaps, Loans, and Escrows

In the dynamic world of blockchain technology, Ripple's XRP Ledger introduces a new paradigm in finance by enabling programmable swaps, loans, and escrows through smart contracts. This transformative capability goes beyond traditional payment systems, providing individuals and businesses with a decentralized and automated framework for executing a variety of financial transactions. This section explores the profound implications of Ripple's approach to programmable financial instruments, shedding light on how the XRP Ledger is reshaping the landscape of swaps, loans, and escrows.

The Power of Programmable Financial Instruments:

Ripple's XRP Ledger distinguishes itself by incorporating smart contract functionality, allowing for the creation of programmable financial instruments. Smart contracts are self-executing contracts with the terms of the agreement directly written into code. This programmability introduces a level of automation and efficiency that transcends traditional financial systems.

Programmable Swaps:

Decentralized and Trustless Asset Exchanges: Programmable swaps on the XRP Ledger represent a decentralized and trustless mechanism for exchanging assets directly on the blockchain. Unlike traditional swaps that often involve intermediaries and centralized clearinghouses, programmable swaps enable users to execute asset exchanges without relying on third parties.

Smart contracts facilitate the execution of swaps by automatically enforcing the terms of the agreement. This decentralized exchange model contributes to enhanced liquidity, reduced counterparty risk, and increased accessibility for a global user base.

Automated Asset Diversification: Programmable swaps empower users to automate asset diversification strategies. For instance, an investor holding a significant amount of one digital asset can use a smart contract to automatically swap a predetermined portion of that asset for another at specified intervals.

This automated approach to asset diversification is particularly valuable in dynamic market conditions, allowing investors to adapt their portfolios without constant manual intervention. It enhances risk management and provides a streamlined mechanism for adjusting asset allocations.

Programmable Loans:

Decentralized Lending Protocols: Programmable loans on the XRP Ledger introduce decentralized lending protocols powered by smart contracts. Users can create lending agreements that automatically enforce terms such as interest rates, repayment schedules, and collateral requirements.

This decentralized lending model eliminates the need for traditional financial intermediaries, enabling peer-to-peer lending on a global scale. Borrowers and lenders can engage directly with one another, fostering financial inclusion and providing access to credit for individuals who may be underserved by traditional banking systems.

Collateralized Lending and Smart Contracts: Smart contracts play a pivotal role in collateralized lending on the XRP Ledger. Borrowers can offer digital assets as collateral, and smart contracts automatically manage the collateralization ratio. In the event of default, the smart contract can initiate the liquidation of collateral to cover outstanding debt.

This automated collateral management enhances the efficiency and transparency of the lending process. Borrowers have access to funds without the need for a traditional credit check, while lenders benefit from reduced default risk through the collateralization of loans.

Programmable Escrows:

Securing Transactions with Smart Contracts: Programmable escrows on the XRP Ledger provide a secure and automated way to facilitate transactions with predefined conditions. Smart contracts act as intermediaries, holding assets in escrow until specific conditions are met. This functionality is particularly valuable in scenarios where trust and security are paramount.

For example, a buyer and seller can use a smart contract escrow to facilitate a transaction. The smart contract holds the buyer's payment in escrow until the seller fulfills the agreed-upon conditions, such as delivering goods or services. Once the conditions are met, the smart contract automatically releases the funds to the seller.

Multi-Signature Escrows: The XRP Ledger supports multi-signature escrows, adding an additional layer of security and flexibility to programmable escrows. Multi-signature escrows require the agreement of multiple parties to release funds, reducing the risk of fraud or misalignment of interests.

This feature is particularly useful in complex transactions involving multiple stakeholders. It ensures that funds are only released when all relevant parties provide their consent, adding an extra layer of trust and security to the escrow process.

Case Study: Decentralized Loan Agreement with Smart Contracts: John, an investor seeking to diversify his digital asset portfolio, decides to participate in a decentralized lending protocol on the XRP Ledger. Using a smart contract, he creates a loan agreement specifying the terms, including the amount, interest rate, and collateral requirements.

Sophia, another participant in the decentralized lending protocol, reviews John's loan terms and decides to lend him the requested amount in XRP. The smart contract automatically locks John's specified collateral in escrow.

Over the loan period, the smart contract manages the repayment schedule and monitors the collateralization ratio. If the collateral value falls below a predetermined threshold, the smart contract can initiate the liquidation of assets to cover potential losses.

Upon successful repayment of the loan, the smart contract releases the collateral back to John, completing the decentralized lending agreement. This process eliminates the need for intermediaries, streamlining the lending experience for both parties.

Challenges and Considerations:

While programmable swaps, loans, and escrows on the XRP Ledger offer unprecedented possibilities, certain challenges and considerations must be addressed:

Regulatory Compliance: Decentralized financial instruments may raise regulatory considerations, particularly in the context of lending and securities laws. Ensuring compliance with diverse regulatory frameworks across jurisdictions is crucial for the widespread adoption of programmable financial instruments.

Smart Contract Security: The security of smart contracts is paramount, as vulnerabilities can lead to exploits and financial losses. Ongoing efforts to enhance the security and auditability of smart contracts on the XRP Ledger are essential to maintain user trust and confidence.

Education and User Awareness: The adoption of programmable financial instruments requires educating users about the advantages and functionalities of these solutions. Building awareness and fostering understanding among users are crucial to ensuring responsible and informed participation in decentralized finance.

Conclusion: Empowering Financial Transactions with Programmable Instruments on the XRP Ledger

Ripple's XRP Ledger, with its integration of programmable swaps, loans, and escrows, stands at the forefront of a transformative shift in how individuals and businesses engage in financial transactions. The inclusion of smart contracts introduces a level of automation and efficiency that transcends traditional financial systems, providing users with unprecedented control over their financial interactions.

As we explore additional facets of Ripple's ecosystem in the following sections, we will uncover the broader implications of these innovations on various industries. The XRP Ledger's role in facilitating programmable financial instruments represents a leap forward in the evolution of decentralized finance, offering individuals and businesses new tools to navigate the complexities of the global financial landscape.

New Economies Built on Decentralized Finance

In the transformative landscape of blockchain technology, Ripple's XRP Ledger plays a pioneering role in fostering new economies built on decentralized finance (DeFi). This groundbreaking capability extends beyond traditional payment systems, opening up avenues for the creation of decentralized financial ecosystems. This section explores the profound implications of Ripple's approach to decentralized finance, shedding light on how the XRP Ledger is catalyzing the emergence of novel economies.

The Evolution of Decentralized Finance:

Decentralized finance, often referred to as DeFi, represents a paradigm shift in the traditional financial landscape. At its core, DeFi seeks to leverage blockchain technology to create open and accessible financial systems that operate without the need for central authorities or intermediaries. Ripple's XRP Ledger, with its integration of smart contracts, contributes to the evolution of decentralized finance by offering a robust and efficient platform for the creation of new economies.

DeFi and the XRP Ledger:

Foundations of a Decentralized Ecosystem: The XRP Ledger serves as the foundation for decentralized finance by providing a secure and decentralized platform for executing financial transactions through smart contracts. Smart contracts enable the creation of programmable financial instruments, facilitating a wide range of activities such as lending, borrowing, trading, and more.

This decentralized ecosystem on the XRP Ledger goes beyond the limitations of traditional financial systems, offering users a borderless and permissionless environment. Participants in this ecosystem have the opportunity to interact directly with one another, eliminating the need for intermediaries and enhancing financial inclusion.

Building New Economies:

Tokenization and Fractional Ownership: Tokenization on the XRP Ledger plays a crucial role in building new economies within the DeFi space. Assets, whether they are real estate, securities, or commodities, can be represented as digital tokens on the blockchain. This process enables fractional ownership, allowing individuals to own and trade fractions of high-value assets.

New economies built on tokenization provide opportunities for a broader range of individuals to participate in asset ownership. Fractional ownership lowers the barrier to entry, enabling users with limited capital to invest in a diverse array of assets and contribute to the creation of decentralized wealth.

Programmable Assets and Smart Contracts: The integration of smart contracts on the XRP Ledger introduces programmable assets, further enriching the possibilities within decentralized economies. These programmable assets can represent dynamic conditions, rules, and functionalities, enabling the creation of sophisticated financial instruments.

Smart contracts automate various processes, including asset swaps, loans, escrows, and more. This automation not only increases the efficiency of financial transactions but also introduces a level of transparency and trust that is inherent to blockchain technology.

Decentralized Exchanges and Liquidity Pools:

Decentralized Exchanges (DEX): Decentralized exchanges on the XRP Ledger contribute to the liquidity and efficiency of decentralized economies. Unlike traditional exchanges that rely on centralized entities to facilitate trades, DEXs operate directly on the blockchain. Users can trade assets directly from their wallets, eliminating the need to deposit funds into a centralized exchange.

The decentralized nature of these exchanges aligns with the principles of blockchain, providing users with greater control over their assets. DEXs contribute to enhanced liquidity, reduced counterparty risk, and increased accessibility for users worldwide.

Liquidity Pools and Automated Market Making (AMM): Liquidity pools, facilitated by smart contracts, play a vital role in decentralized finance on the XRP Ledger. Participants can contribute their assets to liquidity pools, allowing these pools to act as market makers for decentralized exchanges. Automated Market Making (AMM) algorithms automatically adjust asset prices based on supply and demand within the liquidity pool.

This approach enhances liquidity by ensuring that assets are readily available for trading. Participants contributing to liquidity pools receive fees as compensation for their contributions, incentivizing users to actively engage in the decentralized economy.

Decentralized Autonomous Organizations (DAOs):

Community Governance and Decision-Making: Decentralized Autonomous Organizations (DAOs) represent a cornerstone of decentralized economies on the XRP Ledger. DAOs are organizations governed by smart contracts and run on blockchain technology. Participants in DAOs have voting rights proportional to their token holdings, allowing them to collectively make decisions regarding the organization's operations.

DAOs contribute to the decentralization of governance and decision-making processes. This model empowers community members, aligning with the principles of decentralization and providing a framework for collaborative and democratic governance.

Challenges and Considerations:

While the emergence of new economies built on decentralized finance presents exciting opportunities, several challenges and considerations must be addressed:

Regulatory Compliance: The regulatory landscape for decentralized finance is still evolving, and navigating diverse regulatory frameworks across jurisdictions can be challenging. Ensuring compliance with relevant regulations is crucial for the sustainability and widespread adoption of decentralized economies.

Security and Auditing: Security remains a paramount concern in decentralized finance. As the complexity of smart contracts and decentralized applications (DApps) increases, thorough security audits become essential to identify and mitigate vulnerabilities. Ongoing efforts to enhance security measures and conduct regular audits are crucial for maintaining user trust.

User Education and Accessibility: To fully realize the potential of decentralized economies, user education and accessibility must be prioritized. Ensuring that participants understand the functionalities, risks, and benefits of decentralized finance is essential for responsible and informed engagement.

Conclusion: Redefining Finance with Decentralized Economies on the XRP Ledger

Ripple's XRP Ledger, with its integration of smart contracts, stands as a catalyst for the creation of new economies built on decentralized finance. The ability to tokenize assets, leverage programmable financial instruments, and foster decentralized exchanges and organizations represents a paradigm shift in how we perceive and interact with finance.

As we delve deeper into the following sections, exploring additional facets of Ripple's ecosystem, we will uncover the broader implications of these innovations on various industries. The XRP Ledger's role in building new economies within decentralized finance underscores the transformative power of blockchain technology, offering individuals and businesses a decentralized and inclusive alternative to traditional financial systems.

Chapter 7: The Future with the Internet of Value
Internet-Connected World but Not Value

In the interconnected landscape of the modern world, the internet has revolutionized communication, information-sharing, and the way we conduct business. However, a critical gap remains – the seamless transfer and exchange of value. This section delves into the existing disparities between our internet-connected world and the efficient transfer of value, highlighting the challenges that persist in current financial systems and underscoring the need for a paradigm shift towards the Internet of Value.

The Internet's Evolution:

The internet's evolution has been nothing short of revolutionary, reshaping every aspect of our lives. From the early days of simple text-based communication to the multimedia-rich, interconnected world we inhabit today, the internet has become an integral part of our daily existence. It has transformed how we communicate, access information, and conduct business on a global scale.

However, despite this remarkable progress, a significant disconnect exists when it comes to the seamless transfer and exchange of value. While information can be transmitted instantly, the movement of value, particularly in the realm of cross-border payments, remains encumbered by inefficiencies, high costs, and a lack of transparency.

The Disparity:

Instant Information, Delayed Value: In our internet-connected world, information travels at the speed of light. Messages, documents, and data traverse the globe in milliseconds, fostering real-time communication and collaboration. Yet, when it comes to transferring value, the process is often plagued by delays, intermediaries, and archaic systems.

Consider a scenario where a business in one part of the world wants to settle a transaction with a partner in another.

While they can exchange emails, documents, and even conduct video conferences instantly, the actual transfer of funds faces hurdles. Current financial systems, relying on correspondent banking networks and multiple intermediaries, introduce delays that are incongruent with the instantaneous nature of our interconnected world.

High Costs in a Low-Cost Information Era: Another stark contrast lies in the cost dynamics of information transfer versus value transfer. In the digital age, the cost of sending an email or sharing a document online is negligible. Yet, when it comes to cross-border payments, the costs can be exorbitant.

Traditional banking systems involve a series of intermediaries, each levying fees for their services. Currency conversion, transaction fees, and additional charges further contribute to the high costs associated with cross-border payments. This misalignment between the low-cost expectations set by the digital era and the high costs of value transfer highlights a fundamental flaw in current financial infrastructures.

Challenges in Cross-Border Payments:

Inefficiencies and Friction: Cross-border payments face inherent inefficiencies and friction points that hinder the smooth flow of value. The involvement of multiple banks, each with its ledger and settlement process, introduces complexities that contribute to delays and errors. These inefficiencies not only impact the speed of transactions but also result in increased operational costs.

Opaque Processes and Lack of Transparency: The opacity of traditional financial systems is a significant challenge in cross-border payments. Participants often lack visibility into the entire payment process, leading to uncertainties about the status of transactions, associated fees, and the timing of settlements. The lack of transparency creates a trust deficit among participants and increases the risk of errors or disputes.

Limited Financial Inclusion: Current cross-border payment systems pose barriers to financial inclusion. High fees, complex processes, and the reliance on traditional banking structures exclude a substantial portion of the global population from accessing affordable and efficient financial services. The lack of inclusivity perpetuates economic disparities and limits opportunities for individuals and businesses in underserved regions.

Ripple's Vision for the Internet of Value:

Redefining Value Transfer: Ripple envisions a future where the seamless transfer and exchange of value align with the instant communication capabilities of the internet. This vision gives rise to the concept of the Internet of Value (IoV), a paradigm where value can move as freely and effortlessly as information does in our interconnected world.

At the heart of Ripple's vision is the belief that the movement of value should be borderless, instant, and cost-effective. By leveraging blockchain technology and digital assets, Ripple aims to address the disparities between our internet-connected world and the cumbersome processes that characterize current financial systems.

Blockchain and Digital Assets:

Decentralized and Trustless Transactions: Blockchain technology, the underlying foundation of Ripple's vision, enables decentralized and trustless transactions. Instead of relying on a centralized authority or a series of intermediaries, blockchain allows for the direct transfer of value between participants. This decentralization enhances security, reduces the risk of fraud, and eliminates the need for multiple layers of oversight.

Digital Assets as a Medium of Exchange: Digital assets, such as XRP, play a pivotal role in Ripple's vision for the IoV. As a medium of exchange, digital assets can represent value in a form that is natively digital and can be transferred instantly. The use of digital assets eliminates the need for traditional banking structures and enables cross-border transactions to occur directly between parties.

Benefits of the Internet of Value:

Real-Time Settlement: One of the primary benefits of the IoV is real-time settlement. In a world where information travels instantaneously, the transfer of value should be no different. The IoV allows for transactions to settle in real time, providing a level of speed and efficiency that is unparalleled in traditional financial systems.

Reduced Costs and Friction: By eliminating intermediaries and streamlining the settlement process, the IoV significantly reduces costs associated with cross-border payments. Participants can enjoy lower transaction fees, minimal currency conversion costs, and an overall reduction in operational expenses. The IoV aligns with the low-cost expectations set by the digital era.

Enhanced Transparency: Transparency is a cornerstone of the IoV. Participants in value transfers can have complete visibility into the entire transaction lifecycle. From the initiation of a payment to its settlement, users can track the status, associated fees, and any relevant details. This enhanced transparency fosters trust among participants and reduces the risk of errors or disputes.

Use Cases and Implementation:

Santander Bank Implementation: Santander Bank's implementation of Ripple's technology serves as a tangible example of the IoV in action. By leveraging RippleNet, Santander has transformed its cross-border payment processes, offering customers faster and more cost-effective international transfers. The IoV's real-time settlement capabilities have improved the overall customer experience, aligning with the expectations set by our internet-connected world.

MoneyGram's Use of xRapid: MoneyGram's adoption of xRapid, a product within the Ripple ecosystem, exemplifies the IoV's impact on remittances. xRapid leverages the digital asset XRP to provide on-demand liquidity, reducing the need for pre-funded nostro accounts. This innovation has significantly lowered costs for MoneyGram, enabling more affordable and efficient remittances for users.

MercuryFX's Swift Payments: MercuryFX's utilization of Ripple technology for swift payments further demonstrates the IoV's potential. By leveraging Ripple's solutions, MercuryFX has achieved faster payment processing, reduced costs, and increased efficiency in cross-border transactions. The IoV's ability to facilitate quick and transparent value transfers contributes to a more seamless global financial landscape.

The Road Ahead:

Unleashing New Possibilities: The IoV not only addresses existing challenges in cross-border payments but also unleashes new possibilities for how we interact with value. The instantaneous nature of value transfers opens doors to innovative business models, microtransactions, and financial services that were previously impractical.

As blockchain technology and digital assets continue to evolve, the IoV will likely extend its influence beyond cross-border payments. The vision of a seamlessly connected world of value transfer paves the way for broader applications in areas such as trade finance, supply chain management, and beyond.

Global Financial Inclusion: The IoV has the potential to bridge gaps in global financial inclusion. By providing a decentralized and efficient means of transferring value, the IoV empowers individuals and businesses in underserved regions to access affordable and inclusive financial services. This democratization of financial access aligns with the ethos of the internet, which aims to connect and empower people globally.

Collaboration and Standardization: The realization of the IoV requires collaboration among stakeholders and the establishment of standards within the blockchain and financial industries. Interoperability between different blockchain networks and digital asset systems is crucial to creating a truly connected Internet of Value. Standardized protocols and frameworks will facilitate seamless value transfer across diverse platforms, fostering a unified and global IoV ecosystem.

Challenges and Considerations:

Regulatory Evolution: The evolution of regulatory frameworks is essential for the widespread adoption of the IoV. As blockchain and digital assets become integral to the financial landscape, regulators must adapt and establish clear guidelines that ensure compliance, protect consumers, and foster innovation. A harmonized approach to regulation will contribute to the IoV's global acceptance.

Integration with Legacy Systems: While the IoV offers a transformative vision for value transfer, the integration with existing legacy systems poses challenges. Coordinating the transition from traditional financial infrastructures to blockchain-based solutions requires careful planning and collaboration. Hybrid models that bridge the gap between legacy systems and the IoV may be essential during the transition period.

User Education and Adoption: Driving the adoption of the IoV necessitates extensive user education. Individuals, businesses, and financial institutions need to understand the benefits, risks, and functionalities of blockchain-based solutions. Ongoing efforts to enhance user awareness and foster understanding will be crucial for the IoV to reach its full potential.

Conclusion: Transforming Our Connected World into a Connected Value Ecosystem:

Ripple's vision for the Internet of Value represents a monumental shift in how we perceive and interact with value. By aligning the transfer of value with the instantaneous nature of our internet-connected world, the IoV holds the promise of transforming cross-border payments and unlocking new possibilities for financial interactions.

As we explore additional facets of Ripple's ecosystem in the following sections, we will uncover the broader implications of these innovations on various industries. The IoV, with its potential to seamlessly connect the global transfer of value, emerges as a transformative force that transcends traditional financial systems and paves the way for a more connected and inclusive global economy.

RippleNet as the Foundational Internet of Value Network

In the pursuit of transforming our connected world into a seamless ecosystem of value transfer, RippleNet emerges as the foundational network driving the vision of the Internet of Value (IoV). This section explores the pivotal role of RippleNet in realizing the IoV, examining its architecture, key components, and the transformative impact it holds on cross-border payments and the broader financial landscape.

The Imperative for a Foundational Network:

The realization of the Internet of Value hinges on the existence of a robust and interoperable foundational network that can seamlessly facilitate the transfer and exchange of value. RippleNet stands at the forefront of this imperative, offering a decentralized and efficient platform that addresses the limitations of traditional financial systems.

Understanding RippleNet:

RippleNet Architecture: At its core, RippleNet is a decentralized network of financial institutions, payment service providers, and banks that leverage blockchain technology to enable secure, real-time, and cost-effective cross-border payments. RippleNet's architecture is designed to overcome the challenges inherent in traditional correspondent banking systems, introducing a more direct and efficient approach to value transfer.

The architecture of RippleNet consists of three main components: the XRP Ledger, Ripple Consensus Algorithm, and Interledger Protocol (ILP). Together, these components form a cohesive and interoperable network that underpins the IoV vision.

XRP Ledger: The Digital Asset Engine:

At the heart of RippleNet lies the XRP Ledger, a decentralized blockchain that serves as the digital asset engine powering value transfer. XRP, the native digital asset of the XRP Ledger, plays a pivotal role in facilitating on-demand liquidity and bridging different fiat currencies. Unlike traditional settlement processes that rely on pre-funded nostro and vostro accounts, XRP enables instantaneous settlement, minimizing liquidity requirements and reducing costs for participants.

XRP as a Bridge Currency: One of the key innovations of RippleNet is the utilization of XRP as a bridge currency. When two parties want to transact in different fiat currencies, XRP serves as the intermediary, providing a more direct and efficient means of exchanging value. This innovative use of XRP mitigates the need for multiple intermediaries and simplifies the cross-border payment process.

On-Demand Liquidity (ODL): RippleNet leverages XRP to enable On-Demand Liquidity (ODL), a mechanism that transforms the traditional liquidity model. ODL allows participants to source liquidity in real time, eliminating the need for maintaining large pools of pre-funded capital. By leveraging XRP for on-demand liquidity, RippleNet enables faster and more cost-effective cross-border payments, particularly in emerging market corridors.

Ripple Consensus Algorithm: Ensuring Trust and Security:

RippleNet employs a unique consensus algorithm to validate and confirm transactions on the XRP Ledger. Unlike proof-of-work (PoW) mechanisms used in some other blockchain networks, Ripple's consensus algorithm is based on the iterative agreement of network participants. This approach enhances the speed and energy efficiency of the network while maintaining a high level of security and trust.

Validator Nodes: In the Ripple Consensus Algorithm, the network operates through a set of validator nodes that collectively determine the validity and order of transactions. These nodes continuously communicate and share information to achieve consensus on the state of the ledger. The decentralized nature of validator nodes ensures resilience against malicious actors and enhances the overall security of the RippleNet ecosystem.

Transaction Finality: Ripple's consensus algorithm provides fast transaction finality, meaning that once a transaction is confirmed, it is irreversible. This characteristic is crucial for the real-time settlement of cross-border payments, offering participants a high level of certainty and reducing the risk of transaction disputes. The ability to achieve transaction finality rapidly aligns with the IoV's vision of instant value transfer.

Interledger Protocol (ILP): Enabling Interoperability:

Interoperability is a key principle in the IoV, and RippleNet achieves this through the implementation of the Interledger Protocol (ILP). ILP acts as a bridge between different ledgers, whether they are on the XRP Ledger or other blockchain networks, enabling seamless value transfer across diverse systems.

Connecting Ledgers: ILP operates as an open protocol that facilitates interoperability between different ledgers and payment networks. It standardizes the communication between ledgers, allowing them to understand and process transactions from one another. This interoperability is essential for realizing the IoV's vision of a connected network where value can flow freely across various platforms.

Decentralized Architecture: ILP's decentralized architecture aligns with the principles of blockchain technology. It does not rely on a central clearinghouse; instead, it allows participants to connect and transact directly. This decentralized approach contributes to increased efficiency, lower costs, and enhanced security in cross-border payments.

RippleNet's Impact on Cross-Border Payments:

Efficiency Gains and Cost Reduction: RippleNet's architecture, leveraging the XRP Ledger, Ripple Consensus Algorithm, and ILP, brings about significant efficiency gains and cost reductions in cross-border payments. The direct transfer of value between participants, coupled with on-demand liquidity and real-time settlement, streamlines the entire process. This efficiency translates into lower transaction costs, reduced operational expenses, and improved overall economics for participants.

Real-Time Settlement and Enhanced Transparency: RippleNet's focus on real-time settlement addresses a critical gap in traditional correspondent banking systems. The ability to settle transactions instantly, combined with the transparency provided by the XRP Ledger, offers participants unparalleled visibility into the entire payment process. This transparency fosters trust, reduces the risk of errors or disputes, and aligns with the IoV's vision of seamless value transfer.

Global Reach and Financial Inclusion: RippleNet's decentralized and interoperable nature enables participants to connect with a global network of financial institutions. This global reach facilitates enhanced financial inclusion by providing access to efficient and affordable cross-border payment solutions. Individuals and businesses in underserved regions can participate in the global economy, overcoming the barriers imposed by traditional banking systems.

RippleNet in Action: Use Cases and Implementations:

Santander Bank's Implementation: Santander Bank's adoption of RippleNet exemplifies the practical impact of the network on cross-border payments. By leveraging Ripple's technology, Santander has transformed its payment processes, offering customers faster and more cost-effective international transfers. RippleNet's architecture, coupled with the use of XRP for on-demand liquidity, has contributed to a significant improvement in the overall customer experience.

MoneyGram's Use of xRapid: MoneyGram's adoption of xRapid, a product within the Ripple ecosystem, showcases the effectiveness of RippleNet in remittance services. xRapid utilizes XRP to provide on-demand liquidity, reducing the need for pre-funded nostro accounts. This innovation has resulted in lower costs for MoneyGram and has made remittances more affordable and efficient for users.

MercuryFX's Swift Payments: MercuryFX's implementation of Ripple technology for swift payments further underscores the versatility of RippleNet. By leveraging Ripple's solutions, MercuryFX has achieved faster payment processing, reduced costs, and increased efficiency in cross-border transactions. RippleNet's ability to facilitate quick and transparent value transfers contributes to a more seamless global financial landscape.

The Road Ahead for RippleNet and the Internet of Value:

Continued Innovation and Evolution: As technology and the financial landscape continue to evolve, RippleNet remains at the forefront of innovation. Ripple's commitment to ongoing research and development ensures that RippleNet adapts to emerging challenges and incorporates new features that further enhance its capabilities. The evolution of RippleNet contributes to the broader realization of the IoV.

Collaboration and Ecosystem Growth: RippleNet's success is intertwined with the growth of its ecosystem. Continued collaboration with financial institutions, payment service providers, and other stakeholders is essential for expanding RippleNet's reach and impact. The growth of the RippleNet ecosystem contributes to the establishment of a truly interconnected Internet of Value.

Global Regulatory Engagement: The regulatory landscape plays a crucial role in shaping the future of RippleNet and the IoV. Ripple's engagement with global regulators aims to establish clear guidelines and frameworks that promote compliance, consumer protection, and innovation. A collaborative approach to regulation fosters a conducive environment for the widespread adoption of RippleNet and blockchain-based solutions.

Conclusion: RippleNet as the Catalyst for the Internet of Value:

RippleNet stands as the catalyst for realizing the vision of the Internet of Value. Through its decentralized architecture, innovative use of digital assets, and commitment to interoperability, RippleNet addresses the inefficiencies and limitations of traditional cross-border payment systems. The XRP Ledger, Ripple Consensus Algorithm, and Interledger Protocol collectively form a robust foundation that aligns with the principles of the IoV, paving the way for a connected global network of value transfer.

As we explore additional dimensions of Ripple's ecosystem in the following sections, we will uncover how RippleNet's transformative impact extends beyond cross-border payments. The foundational role of RippleNet in shaping the Internet of Value underscores its significance in reshaping the future of financial interactions on a global scale.

True Real-Time Settlement between Ledgers

In the pursuit of an interconnected and seamless global transfer of value, the concept of true real-time settlement between ledgers stands as a cornerstone of the Internet of Value (IoV). This section delves into the significance of achieving instantaneous settlement in cross-border payments, explores the challenges posed by traditional systems, and elucidates how Ripple's innovative approach, particularly through RippleNet, is reshaping the landscape by enabling true real-time settlement.

The Imperative for Real-Time Settlement:

The traditional settlement process in cross-border payments involves a series of intermediaries, multiple ledgers, and a significant time lag before funds are successfully transferred and settled. This delay has long been a pain point for businesses and individuals engaged in international transactions, giving rise to the need for a paradigm shift towards real-time settlement.

Understanding the Traditional Settlement Process:

Inefficiencies in Traditional Systems: Traditional cross-border payment systems often rely on a web of correspondent banks, each maintaining its ledger and settlement process. When a payment is initiated, it passes through these intermediaries, with each institution updating its ledger to reflect the transaction. This sequential process introduces delays, as each intermediary may take time to confirm and settle the transaction.

The Nostro and Vostro Account Conundrum: One of the primary contributors to settlement delays is the reliance on pre-funded accounts, known as nostro and vostro accounts. In the traditional correspondent banking model, financial institutions maintain these accounts in each other's currencies to facilitate cross-border payments. However, maintaining these accounts ties up capital and requires careful management to ensure liquidity for transactions.

Currency Conversion Challenges: In a global economy where currencies vary, the need for currency conversion further complicates the settlement process. Each intermediary along the payment route may engage in currency conversion, leading to additional delays and costs. The lack of synchronization and real-time visibility across different ledgers exacerbates these challenges.

The Vision of True Real-Time Settlement:

Instantaneous Value Transfer: The vision of true real-time settlement in the IoV revolves around the instantaneous transfer and settlement of value. Unlike the delayed and sequential processes of traditional systems, true real-time settlement envisions a scenario where transactions settle instantly as they occur, eliminating the need for intermediaries to confirm and update ledgers.

Alignment with Digital Era Expectations: In an age where information travels instantly, the expectation for the transfer of value to occur just as rapidly is a natural progression. True real-time settlement aligns with the principles of immediacy and efficiency that define the digital era. It not only addresses the frustrations associated with delayed settlements but also opens doors to new possibilities in business models, financial services, and global trade.

Challenges Addressed by Ripple's Approach:

On-Demand Liquidity with XRP: Ripple's approach to achieving true real-time settlement is exemplified by its use of XRP as a bridge currency in the settlement process. On-Demand Liquidity (ODL), a solution within the Ripple ecosystem, leverages XRP to provide instant liquidity for cross-border transactions. Instead of relying on pre-funded nostro accounts, financial institutions can use XRP to source liquidity on-demand, reducing the need for maintaining large pools of capital.

XRP as a Bridge Currency: XRP's role as a bridge currency in the settlement process is pivotal to achieving true real-time settlement. When two parties engage in cross-border transactions involving different fiat currencies, XRP serves as the intermediary that bridges the gap. This innovative use of XRP enables direct and instant exchanges between fiat currencies, eliminating the delays associated with traditional settlement methods.

The RippleNet Advantage:

RippleNet's Decentralized Architecture: RippleNet, with its decentralized architecture, plays a crucial role in facilitating true real-time settlement. The network connects a diverse range of financial institutions, payment service providers, and banks, enabling them to transact directly with one another. This direct interaction, facilitated by RippleNet, reduces the number of intermediaries involved in the settlement process and contributes to the efficiency of value transfer.

The XRP Ledger's Consensus Algorithm: The Ripple Consensus Algorithm, employed by the XRP Ledger, ensures the validity and finality of transactions in near real-time. Unlike the extended settlement periods of traditional systems, transactions on the XRP Ledger achieve rapid consensus, providing participants with confidence in the swift and irreversible nature of settlements.

Interledger Protocol (ILP) for Interoperability: Interoperability is a key aspect of achieving true real-time settlement between ledgers. RippleNet incorporates the Interledger Protocol (ILP), which acts as a bridge between different ledgers and payment networks. ILP standardizes the communication between diverse systems, allowing for seamless value transfer across various platforms. This interoperability is instrumental in realizing the interconnected vision of the IoV.

RippleNet in Action: True Real-Time Settlement Use Cases:

Santander Bank's Swift International Payments: Santander Bank's implementation of RippleNet showcases the practical impact of true real-time settlement. By leveraging Ripple's technology, Santander has streamlined its international payment processes, offering customers the ability to send and receive funds with unprecedented speed. The elimination of delays associated with traditional settlement systems aligns with the expectations set by true real-time settlement.

MoneyGram's Efficient Remittances with xRapid: MoneyGram's adoption of xRapid, a solution within the Ripple ecosystem, illustrates the efficiency gains achieved through true real-time settlement. xRapid utilizes XRP to provide on-demand liquidity for remittances, allowing MoneyGram to settle transactions in real time. This innovative approach not only reduces costs but also transforms the remittance experience for users by providing faster and more reliable transfers.

MercuryFX's Swift Payments with Ripple Technology: MercuryFX's utilization of Ripple technology for swift payments further exemplifies the advantages of true real-time settlement. By leveraging RippleNet, MercuryFX has achieved faster payment processing and reduced settlement times in cross-border transactions. The enhanced efficiency translates into a more seamless global financial landscape for both businesses and individuals.

The Broader Implications for Global Finance:

Unlocking New Business Models: True real-time settlement has the potential to unlock new business models that were previously hindered by the delays and complexities of traditional settlement processes. Businesses can explore innovative payment solutions, such as microtransactions, real-time supply chain financing, and instant settlement of trade transactions. The ability to settle transactions instantly opens doors to a myriad of possibilities across industries.

Microtransactions and Instant Settlement: The efficiency of true real-time settlement enables microtransactions to become a viable and scalable business model. Whether it's in the realm of digital content, gaming, or small-scale financial transactions, the ability to settle payments instantly enhances the feasibility of microtransactions. This opens up new revenue streams and business opportunities that align with the growing trend of digital microeconomies.

Enhanced Risk Management: Traditional settlement processes, with their extended settlement periods, expose participants to various risks, including currency fluctuation and counterparty risk. True real-time settlement mitigates these risks by reducing the time between initiation and settlement. This enhanced risk management is particularly valuable for businesses engaged in global trade and finance, where timely settlements are critical.

Challenges and Considerations:

Regulatory Alignment: Achieving true real-time settlement requires regulatory frameworks that support the adoption of innovative technologies and digital assets. Regulators play a crucial role in ensuring compliance, consumer protection, and the stability of financial systems. Collaboration between the private sector and regulatory bodies is essential to address the evolving challenges and foster an environment conducive to true real-time settlement.

Integration with Legacy Systems: The transition from traditional settlement systems to true real-time settlement poses integration challenges. Existing legacy systems may need to be adapted or replaced to accommodate the speed and efficiency of true real-time settlement. Hybrid models that bridge the gap between legacy systems and innovative solutions may be essential during this transition period.

User Education and Trust: As with any transformative shift, user education and trust-building are crucial elements for the widespread adoption of true real-time settlement. Businesses, financial institutions, and individuals need to understand the benefits, risks, and functionalities of the new settlement paradigm. Efforts to enhance user awareness and foster trust will play a pivotal role in the successful implementation of true real-time settlement solutions.

Conclusion: Redefining Global Value Transfer with True Real-Time Settlement:

In conclusion, true real-time settlement between ledgers represents a paradigm shift in the way we perceive and conduct cross-border payments. Ripple's approach, as exemplified by RippleNet, leverages innovative technologies such as XRP, the Ripple Consensus Algorithm, and the Interledger Protocol to address the inefficiencies of traditional settlement processes.

The vision of the Internet of Value is inexorably linked with the achievement of true real-time settlement. As we explore additional facets of Ripple's ecosystem in the following sections, we will uncover the broader implications of these innovations on various industries. True real-time settlement, with its potential to redefine global value transfer, emerges as a key enabler for a more connected, efficient, and inclusive global economy.

Applications We Can't Yet Envision

In the ever-evolving landscape of technology and finance, the concept of the Internet of Value (IoV) heralds a future where value transfer is not only seamless but also opens up possibilities that extend beyond our current understanding. This section delves into the realm of applications we can't yet envision, exploring the transformative potential of RippleNet and the IoV in shaping industries, economies, and societal interactions.

The Unpredictable Nature of Technological Evolution:

One of the fascinating aspects of technological evolution is its unpredictable trajectory. As new innovations emerge, they often give rise to applications and use cases that were not initially foreseen. The IoV, with its foundational network RippleNet, serves as a catalyst for such unforeseen applications by providing a decentralized and efficient platform for value transfer. As we explore the potential applications we can't yet envision, it's essential to recognize the dynamic nature of technology and its capacity to reshape our world in unexpected ways.

Enabling Innovation Through RippleNet:

RippleNet as a Catalyst for Innovation: RippleNet, with its decentralized architecture, real-time settlement capabilities, and interoperability, acts as a catalyst for innovation in the financial and payment industry. By addressing the inefficiencies of traditional cross-border payment systems, RippleNet opens the door to new possibilities and applications that leverage the IoV's principles of immediacy, efficiency, and connectivity.

Decentralization and Empowerment: The decentralization inherent in RippleNet empowers a diverse range of participants, from financial institutions to individual users, to transact directly and securely. This shift in power dynamics fosters an environment where innovation can flourish, unburdened by the constraints of centralized control. Applications that empower users, promote financial inclusion, and redefine traditional business models are likely to emerge in this decentralized landscape.

Exploring Unforeseen Applications:

Microtransactions Reshaping Digital Economies: One potential application that the IoV could unlock is the widespread adoption of microtransactions on a global scale. The efficiency and low transaction costs facilitated by RippleNet may pave the way for new digital economies based on microtransactions. From small payments for digital content to instant settlements in online gaming, the IoV could catalyze the growth of microeconomies that were previously impractical due to transaction fees and settlement delays.

Tokenization of Real-world Assets: The IoV has the potential to enable the tokenization of real-world assets, a concept where physical assets such as real estate, art, or even commodities are represented digitally on a blockchain. This tokenization could facilitate fractional ownership, making it easier for individuals to invest in high-value assets. The seamless transfer of tokenized assets on the IoV may lead to the creation of new investment opportunities and liquidity in traditionally illiquid markets.

Decentralized Finance (DeFi) Beyond Current Models: While decentralized finance (DeFi) is gaining traction, the IoV could take it a step further by introducing innovative DeFi models that leverage real-time settlement and interoperability. Smart contracts on the IoV may enable more complex financial instruments, programmable lending, and decentralized exchanges that operate seamlessly across different blockchain networks. The IoV's potential to redefine the DeFi landscape lies in its ability to connect diverse financial ecosystems.

Cross-Industry Transformations:

Supply Chain Traceability and Transparency: The IoV, with its emphasis on transparency and real-time settlement, could revolutionize supply chain management. By leveraging

RippleNet's interoperability and the immutability of blockchain, supply chains could achieve unprecedented levels of traceability. Each step in the supply chain, from production to delivery, could be recorded on a decentralized ledger, ensuring authenticity, reducing fraud, and providing consumers with real-time information about the products they purchase.

Healthcare Data Security and Interoperability: In the realm of healthcare, the IoV could play a transformative role in securing patient data and enhancing interoperability among healthcare systems. Blockchain technology, coupled with RippleNet's decentralized architecture, could facilitate secure and transparent sharing of medical records across different healthcare providers. Patients could have more control over their data, and healthcare providers could access real-time, accurate information, leading to improved patient care.

Efficient Energy Trading in a Decentralized Grid: As the world transitions to decentralized energy grids, the IoV could facilitate efficient energy trading among consumers and producers. Blockchain-based smart contracts on the IoV could enable peer-to-peer energy transactions in real-time, allowing consumers with excess energy to sell it directly to others in their community. This decentralized approach to energy trading aligns with the growing trend towards renewable energy and community-driven sustainability initiatives.

Challenges and Considerations:

Regulatory Adaptation to Unforeseen Applications: The emergence of applications we can't yet envision poses challenges for regulators in adapting to new paradigms. Regulatory frameworks may need to evolve to address the complexities and risks associated with unforeseen applications on the IoV. Collaborative efforts between the private sector, regulators, and policymakers will be essential to strike a balance between fostering innovation and ensuring compliance.

Security and Privacy Concerns: With new and unforeseen applications come heightened security and privacy concerns. Innovations in the IoV may involve the exchange of sensitive information and assets, requiring robust security measures to safeguard against cyber threats and unauthorized access. Striking a balance between transparency and privacy will be crucial in maintaining the integrity of the IoV.

User Education and Adoption: The successful adoption of unforeseen applications on the IoV hinges on user education and awareness. Users, whether individuals or businesses, need to understand the benefits, risks, and functionalities of these new applications. Efforts to educate and guide users will play a pivotal role in ensuring a smooth transition and widespread acceptance of innovative IoV applications.

Conclusion: Anticipating the Unanticipated in the Internet of Value:

The concept of applications we can't yet envision encapsulates the dynamic and unpredictable nature of technological evolution. RippleNet, as the foundational network of the IoV, provides the infrastructure for innovations that extend beyond our current understanding. Whether it's reshaping digital economies through microtransactions, enabling the tokenization of real-world assets, or transforming cross-industry processes, the IoV holds the potential to unlock possibilities that may surprise us in the coming years.

As we navigate the uncharted territory of applications we can't yet envision, the principles of decentralization, transparency, and real-time settlement embedded in RippleNet will continue to serve as guiding lights. The collaborative efforts of industry stakeholders, regulators, and the broader community will be instrumental in realizing the full potential of the IoV and the unforeseen applications that await us on this transformative journey.

Conclusion
Key Innovations of RippleNet and XRP

In the ever-evolving landscape of financial technology, RippleNet and its native digital asset, XRP, stand as pioneers that have revolutionized the way we perceive and execute cross-border payments. This conclusion explores the key innovations brought forth by RippleNet and XRP, examining their transformative impact on the financial industry, addressing challenges, and envisioning a future where value transfer is seamless, efficient, and accessible to all.

The RippleNet Ecosystem: A Paradigm Shift in Cross-Border Payments

Redefining Cross-Border Payments: One of the key innovations introduced by RippleNet is the redefinition of cross-border payments. Traditionally, such transactions were marred by inefficiencies, including delays, high costs, and opacity. RippleNet's decentralized architecture, powered by blockchain technology, eliminates the need for multiple intermediaries and provides a direct and secure channel for financial institutions to transact with one another. This innovation has streamlined cross-border payments, making them faster, more cost-effective, and transparent.

Real-Time Settlement: Perhaps one of the most groundbreaking innovations is RippleNet's ability to facilitate real-time settlement. The traditional settlement process in cross-border payments involved a series of intermediaries and delays, often taking days to complete. RippleNet's decentralized ledger, coupled with the XRP Ledger's consensus algorithm, enables transactions to be settled in near real-time. This not only addresses the liquidity challenges associated with traditional nostro and vostro accounts but also enhances the overall efficiency of global value transfer.

On-Demand Liquidity with XRP: XRP, as the native digital asset of RippleNet, plays a pivotal role in introducing on-demand liquidity to cross-border transactions. Traditionally, financial institutions maintained pre-funded accounts in various currencies to facilitate international payments. With XRP, on-demand liquidity allows these institutions to source liquidity dynamically, reducing the need for holding large amounts of capital in different fiat currencies. This innovation significantly minimizes costs, unlocks trapped capital, and provides a more efficient mechanism for cross-border liquidity.

Empowering Financial Institutions:

RippleNet's Network of Networks: The concept of RippleNet as a network of networks signifies a paradigm shift in how financial institutions connect and transact globally. RippleNet serves as a unifying force that brings together a diverse array of payment service providers, banks, and financial institutions. This interconnected network empowers participants to transact directly, eliminating the need for multiple correspondent banking relationships. Financial institutions can now expand their reach, offer enhanced services, and explore new business opportunities through a single connection to RippleNet.

Standardized Technology and Rules: RippleNet introduces a standardized approach to technology and rules, providing a common framework for participants. In traditional cross-border payments, each financial institution might operate on different technology stacks and adhere to varied rules and processes. RippleNet's standardized infrastructure streamlines communication and transactions, fostering a level playing field for all participants. This standardization enhances interoperability and ensures a consistent experience across the RippleNet ecosystem.

XRP: A Bridge Currency and Catalyst for Efficiency

Bridge Currency Facilitating Liquidity: XRP's role as a bridge currency is a distinctive feature that sets it apart from traditional fiat currencies in cross-border transactions. When financial institutions need to transact between different fiat currencies, XRP serves as the intermediary, facilitating instant and cost-effective exchanges. This innovative use of a digital asset as a bridge currency not only accelerates the settlement process but also reduces reliance on pre-funded accounts, leading to greater liquidity efficiency.

Cost Reduction and Capital Unlocking: One of the key innovations brought by XRP is the significant reduction in transaction costs associated with cross-border payments. By using XRP as a bridge currency, financial institutions can minimize the costs associated with multiple currency conversions and intermediary fees. Moreover, the on-demand liquidity enabled by XRP allows institutions to unlock capital that would otherwise be tied up in pre-funded accounts. This capital efficiency enhances the overall financial health of participating institutions.

Interoperability and Integration:

Interledger Protocol (ILP): Interoperability is a cornerstone of RippleNet's innovations, and the Interledger Protocol (ILP) plays a crucial role in achieving seamless connectivity. ILP serves as a bridge between different ledgers and payment networks, standardizing communication protocols. This interoperability enables transactions to flow effortlessly across diverse platforms, fostering a connected and inclusive financial ecosystem. RippleNet's adherence to ILP ensures that participants can transact with each other, regardless of their underlying technologies.

Integration with Legacy Systems: Recognizing the importance of seamless integration with existing financial infrastructure, RippleNet is designed to integrate with legacy systems. Financial institutions can adopt RippleNet without the need for a complete overhaul of their current systems. This pragmatic approach to integration ensures a smooth transition for participants, allowing them to leverage the benefits of RippleNet without disrupting their existing operations. The ability to integrate with legacy systems sets RippleNet apart as a practical solution for the evolving needs of the financial industry.

Real-World Implementations and Industry Impact:

Santander Bank's Implementation: Santander Bank's adoption of RippleNet for international payments exemplifies the real-world impact of these innovations. By leveraging RippleNet's standardized technology and rules, Santander has streamlined its global payment processes. The use of XRP as a bridge currency has allowed Santander to achieve faster settlement times and minimize transaction costs, providing an enhanced experience for both the bank and its customers.

MoneyGram's Utilization of xRapid: MoneyGram's implementation of xRapid, a solution within the Ripple ecosystem that utilizes XRP, showcases the transformative potential of on-demand liquidity. By leveraging XRP, MoneyGram has significantly reduced the costs associated with liquidity provision for cross-border payments. xRapid's real-time settlement capability has not only improved the efficiency of MoneyGram's remittance services but has also set a precedent for the wider adoption of digital assets in the traditional financial space.

MercuryFX's Swift Payments with Ripple Technology: MercuryFX's utilization of Ripple technology for swift payments underscores the broad applicability of RippleNet's innovations. The company has experienced faster payment processing and reduced settlement times, highlighting the efficiency gains that can be achieved through Ripple's decentralized infrastructure. MercuryFX's success story serves as a testament to the adaptability of RippleNet across diverse use cases and financial scenarios.

Beyond Payments: Unleashing the Potential of RippleNet and XRP

Smart Contracts and NFTs: While RippleNet's primary focus is on cross-border payments, the innovations introduced by XRP extend beyond traditional financial transactions. RippleNet's infrastructure, coupled with the XRP Ledger's capabilities, opens doors to the integration of smart contracts and non-fungible tokens (NFTs). This expansion of functionality positions RippleNet as a versatile platform that can support a broader range of financial instruments and digital assets.

Programmable Swaps, Loans, and Escrows: The programmability of the XRP Ledger enables the creation of advanced financial instruments such as programmable swaps, loans, and escrows. These capabilities go beyond traditional payment systems, allowing participants to engage in more complex financial arrangements with programmable conditions. RippleNet's support for such programmable financial instruments contributes to the evolution of decentralized finance (DeFi) and the creation of innovative financial products.

New Economies Built on Decentralized Finance: RippleNet's role in facilitating decentralized finance (DeFi) extends beyond its impact on cross-border payments. The platform's support for programmable financial instruments, coupled with the efficiency gains brought by XRP, contributes to the broader trend of building new economies on decentralized finance principles. RippleNet becomes a cornerstone for the development of decentralized applications (dApps) and financial ecosystems that operate on blockchain technology.

The Future with the Internet of Value: Shaping a Connected World

Internet Connected World but Not Value: In envisioning the future with the Internet of Value (IoV), RippleNet emerges as a foundational network that addresses the disparity between the connectedness of the internet and the inefficiencies in value transfer. The IoV, championed by RippleNet and XRP, seeks to create a seamlessly connected global economy where the transfer of value is as immediate and accessible as the exchange of information.

RippleNet as Foundational IoV Network: RippleNet's positioning as a foundational IoV network signifies its pivotal role in shaping the future of global value transfer. The IoV, envisioned as a network where value moves as freely as information, relies on decentralized and interoperable systems. RippleNet, with its emphasis on real-time settlement, standardized technology, and interoperability, embodies the principles necessary to establish the IoV as a reality.

True Real-Time Settlement Between Ledgers: A key innovation propelling the IoV forward is the achievement of true real-time settlement between ledgers. Traditional financial systems often suffer from settlement delays and discrepancies between ledgers. RippleNet's decentralized approach, coupled with the efficiency of XRP, addresses these challenges by enabling true real-time settlement. This innovation not only enhances the speed of cross-border transactions but also paves the way for a more connected and synchronized global financial ecosystem.

Applications We Can't Yet Envision: Unleashing the Unforeseen Potential

The Unpredictable Nature of Technological Evolution: As we anticipate the applications we can't yet envision, it's crucial to acknowledge the unpredictable nature of technological evolution. The IoV, powered by RippleNet and XRP, introduces a dynamic ecosystem where innovations may emerge in ways that challenge our current understanding. The evolution of technology often gives rise to applications and use cases that were not initially foreseen, making the IoV a fertile ground for transformative and unforeseen developments.

Conclusion: Navigating the Roadmap to the Future of Value Transfer

Roadmap to the Future of Value Transfer: In conclusion, the journey mapped by RippleNet and XRP represents a roadmap to the future of value transfer. From redefining cross-border payments to enabling on-demand liquidity, fostering interoperability, and extending beyond payments to support smart contracts and decentralized finance, RippleNet and XRP have reshaped the financial landscape.

Continuing to Evolve and Expand: As technology and financial ecosystems continue to evolve, RippleNet remains at the forefront of innovation. The commitment to real-time settlement, interoperability, and efficiency positions RippleNet as a driving force in the ongoing transformation of global finance. The collaboration between financial institutions, regulators, and the broader community will play a pivotal role in navigating the challenges and embracing the opportunities that lie ahead.

Key Innovations of RippleNet and XRP: A Transformative Legacy

In reflecting on the key innovations of RippleNet and XRP, it becomes evident that their impact extends far beyond the realm of cross-border payments. RippleNet's network of networks, real-time settlement capabilities, and interoperability, combined with XRP's role as a bridge currency and catalyst for efficiency, have laid the foundation for a future where the transfer of value is efficient, accessible, and innovative.

As we stand at the intersection of the present and the future, the legacy of RippleNet and XRP is marked by a transformative journey—a journey that has not only addressed the inefficiencies of traditional finance but has also unlocked unforeseen possibilities. From applications that redefine digital economies to the establishment of the Internet of Value, RippleNet and XRP continue to shape the roadmap to a connected, efficient, and inclusive global financial ecosystem.

Continuing to Evolve and Expand

In the dynamic landscape of financial technology, adaptation and evolution are not mere aspirations but prerequisites for sustained relevance. As we conclude our exploration of RippleNet's transformative journey and the pivotal role played by XRP, it is imperative to cast our gaze towards the future. This section delves into the trajectory of continued evolution and expansion, examining the factors that will shape the ongoing narrative of RippleNet and XRP.

Embracing Technological Advancements:

Blockchain and Distributed Ledger Technology: The cornerstone of RippleNet's innovations lies in the utilization of blockchain and distributed ledger technology. As these technologies continue to advance, RippleNet is poised to benefit from increased scalability, security enhancements, and improved consensus mechanisms. Embracing the latest developments in blockchain ensures that RippleNet remains at the forefront of decentralized finance, providing a robust and secure infrastructure for cross-border payments and beyond.

Integration of Quantum Computing: The advent of quantum computing presents both challenges and opportunities for the fintech industry. While quantum computers pose a potential threat to cryptographic systems, they also open avenues for new, quantum-resistant algorithms. The continuous evolution of RippleNet includes staying abreast of developments in quantum-resistant cryptography, ensuring the platform's resilience against emerging threats and maintaining the security of cross-border transactions.

Navigating Regulatory Landscapes:

Adaptation to Regulatory Changes: The regulatory landscape for cryptocurrencies and blockchain technology is dynamic and subject to constant evolution. RippleNet's ability to navigate and adapt to regulatory changes will be instrumental in ensuring compliance and fostering collaboration with regulatory bodies. Proactive engagement with regulators, policymakers, and industry stakeholders is essential for maintaining a conducive environment for the continued expansion of RippleNet.

Global Regulatory Frameworks: As cross-border payments transcend geographical boundaries, RippleNet must engage with the development of global regulatory frameworks. Collaborative efforts between countries and international organizations are crucial to establishing standardized regulations that facilitate seamless and compliant cross-border transactions. RippleNet's commitment to adherence to global regulatory standards positions it as a responsible and trustworthy participant in the evolving financial ecosystem.

Fostering Collaborative Partnerships:

Expansion of RippleNet Partnerships: The strength of RippleNet lies in its network of diverse participants, including financial institutions, payment service providers, and technology companies. Ongoing expansion and diversification of RippleNet partnerships are critical for broadening the platform's reach and impact. Collaborating with entities from various sectors enhances interoperability and opens doors to innovative use cases beyond traditional financial transactions.

Engaging with Central Banks: Engagement with central banks is increasingly becoming a focal point for fintech platforms. RippleNet's evolution includes fostering relationships with central banks to explore the integration of digital currencies and central bank digital currencies (CBDCs). Collaborative efforts with central banks can contribute to the establishment of a more efficient and interconnected global payment infrastructure.

Technological Enhancements and Research Initiatives:

Research and Development Initiatives: Investing in research and development is a fundamental aspect of RippleNet's continued evolution. Research initiatives can explore innovative applications of blockchain technology, enhancements to the consensus algorithm, and the integration of emerging technologies. This commitment to R&D ensures that RippleNet remains at the forefront of technological advancements, driving the evolution of cross-border payments and financial services.

Exploration of Interoperability Solutions: Interoperability remains a key theme in the evolution of blockchain-based platforms. RippleNet's exploration of interoperability solutions, both within its ecosystem and with external networks, is crucial for fostering seamless connectivity. Efforts to standardize protocols and enhance interoperability contribute to the creation of a more interconnected and inclusive financial landscape.

Environmental and Social Responsibility:

Sustainability in Blockchain Operations: As environmental concerns gain prominence, the evolution of RippleNet includes a commitment to sustainability in blockchain operations. Exploring energy-efficient consensus mechanisms and adopting eco-friendly practices contribute to minimizing the environmental footprint of blockchain networks. Environmental responsibility aligns RippleNet with global sustainability goals and enhances its reputation as a socially conscious fintech platform.

Financial Inclusion Initiatives: The expansion of RippleNet goes hand in hand with initiatives aimed at fostering financial inclusion. RippleNet's role in facilitating low-cost, real-time transactions has the potential to bridge the gap for unbanked and underbanked populations. Collaborating with financial institutions, governments, and non-profit organizations can drive initiatives that empower individuals in underserved regions, bringing them into the global financial ecosystem.

User Education and Awareness:

Empowering Users with Knowledge: The success of RippleNet's continued evolution relies on empowering users with knowledge and fostering awareness of the platform's capabilities.

Education initiatives aimed at financial institutions, businesses, and individual users can demystify blockchain technology, clarify the benefits of RippleNet, and address any misconceptions. Informed users are more likely to embrace the platform, contributing to its sustained growth.

Enhanced Security Measures: With the persistent evolution of cybersecurity threats, enhancing security measures is a perpetual priority. RippleNet's commitment to user security includes the adoption of state-of-the-art encryption, multi-factor authentication, and continuous monitoring systems. Collaborative efforts with cybersecurity experts and organizations contribute to fortifying RippleNet's defenses against evolving threats.

Conclusion: A Roadmap Unfolding

In conclusion, the journey of RippleNet and XRP is not a finite narrative but an unfolding roadmap characterized by adaptability, innovation, and a commitment to shaping the future of cross-border payments. As the platform continues to evolve and expand, it navigates a complex landscape of technological advancements, regulatory dynamics, and global partnerships.

The vision of RippleNet extends beyond being a facilitator of cross-border payments; it aspires to be a catalyst for a more interconnected, efficient, and inclusive global financial ecosystem. The ongoing evolution of RippleNet, coupled with the intrinsic capabilities of XRP, positions this fintech platform as a transformative force in the journey towards redefining the way value is transferred on a global scale.

As RippleNet and XRP traverse this roadmap, the collaborative efforts of stakeholders, the foresight of innovators, and the adaptability to emerging trends will be pivotal. The narrative of RippleNet's evolution is an open chapter, with each phase contributing to the broader story of a decentralized, efficient, and accessible future for global finance.

Roadmap to the Future of Value Transfer

In the culmination of our exploration into the transformative journey of RippleNet and the pivotal role played by XRP, we turn our attention to the roadmap that charts the future of value transfer. This section navigates the key elements that constitute this roadmap, examining the principles, innovations, and collaborative efforts that will shape the trajectory of RippleNet and XRP in redefining the landscape of global finance.

Principles Guiding the Roadmap:

Decentralization as a Cornerstone: The roadmap to the future of value transfer is underpinned by the principle of decentralization. RippleNet's commitment to decentralization signifies a departure from traditional financial models dominated by central authorities. This shift empowers participants, reduces reliance on intermediaries, and enhances the security and transparency of transactions. As RippleNet continues to evolve, maintaining and reinforcing its decentralized architecture will be instrumental in shaping a more resilient and inclusive financial ecosystem.

Transparency and Trust: Transparency is a guiding beacon on the roadmap, fostering trust among participants in the RippleNet ecosystem. Blockchain technology, with its immutable and transparent ledger, ensures that every transaction is traceable and verifiable. Upholding and enhancing transparency will remain a priority, instilling confidence in financial institutions, businesses, and users engaging in cross-border transactions. Trust is the bedrock upon which the future of value transfer is built.

Innovation as a Catalyst: Innovation serves as a catalyst propelling the roadmap forward. The future of value transfer is intrinsically linked to the ability of RippleNet and XRP to innovate continually. From real-time settlement to on-demand liquidity and beyond, embracing emerging technologies, exploring novel use cases, and pushing the boundaries of what is possible will define the trajectory of this innovation-driven roadmap.

Technological Advancements:

Blockchain Evolution: The roadmap acknowledges the dynamic evolution of blockchain technology. As RippleNet continues its journey, staying abreast of advancements in blockchain is imperative. Scalability, interoperability, and sustainability are key areas of focus. The integration of second-layer solutions, consensus algorithm enhancements, and advancements in smart contract capabilities contribute to the technological robustness of RippleNet.

Integration of Emerging Technologies: Beyond blockchain, the future of value transfer explores the integration of emerging technologies. Artificial intelligence, machine learning, and quantum computing are on the horizon, presenting opportunities to enhance security, optimize transaction processing, and address challenges associated with cryptographic systems. Integrating these technologies into the RippleNet ecosystem positions it at the forefront of technological innovation in the financial sector.

Global Collaboration and Regulatory Frameworks:

Collaborative Partnerships: Global collaboration emerges as a cornerstone of the roadmap. RippleNet's expansion relies on fostering collaborative partnerships with financial institutions, central banks, technology companies, and regulatory bodies. These partnerships contribute to the establishment of a more interconnected and interoperable financial network. Through alliances that transcend borders, RippleNet can extend its reach and impact, ensuring a seamless flow of value on a global scale.

Adaptation to Regulatory Dynamics: The roadmap recognizes the importance of adapting to regulatory dynamics. As the regulatory landscape for cryptocurrencies and blockchain evolves, RippleNet's compliance with global standards becomes paramount. Proactive engagement with regulators, participation in shaping regulatory frameworks, and adherence to compliance standards ensure that RippleNet remains a responsible and sustainable participant in the financial ecosystem.

Financial Inclusion and Social Impact:

Empowering the Unbanked: Financial inclusion is a key waypoint on the roadmap. RippleNet's capability to facilitate low-cost, real-time transactions holds the potential to empower the unbanked and underbanked populations. Collaborative initiatives with governments, NGOs, and financial institutions can drive efforts to extend the benefits of RippleNet to individuals in underserved regions, bridging the gap between the connected and the unconnected.

Sustainable and Socially Responsible Practices: Sustainability and social responsibility form integral components of the roadmap. RippleNet's commitment to eco-friendly blockchain operations and ethical business practices aligns with the growing emphasis on environmental and social impact. As the financial sector evolves, the roadmap envisions RippleNet as a leader in championing sustainable practices and contributing to positive societal outcomes.

User Education and Adoption:

Demystifying Blockchain for Users: User education emerges as a crucial element of the roadmap. Demystifying blockchain technology, clarifying the benefits of RippleNet, and addressing any misconceptions foster a user base that is informed and confident in utilizing the platform. Educational initiatives targeted at financial institutions, businesses, and individual users contribute to the widespread adoption of RippleNet and XRP.

Enhancing User Experience: The roadmap places a spotlight on enhancing the user experience. Streamlining user interfaces, optimizing transaction processes, and incorporating user feedback contribute to a user-centric ecosystem. As RippleNet evolves, prioritizing user experience ensures that participants find value in the platform, fostering loyalty and sustained engagement.

Strategic Expansion Beyond Payments:

Diversification of Use Cases: Beyond payments, the roadmap envisions a diversification of use cases for RippleNet. The integration of smart contracts, tokenization of assets, and the exploration of decentralized finance (DeFi) contribute to the expansion of RippleNet's functionalities. This diversification positions RippleNet as a versatile platform capable of supporting a broad spectrum of financial instruments and applications.

Integration of XRP in Various Industries: XRP's role extends beyond being a bridge currency for cross-border payments. The roadmap includes the integration of XRP in various industries and sectors. From facilitating tokenized assets to enabling programmable financial instruments, XRP becomes a catalyst for innovation in areas such as supply chain finance, healthcare, and entertainment.

Roadmap to the Internet of Value (IoV):

Foundational Network for IoV: The roadmap converges with the vision of RippleNet as a foundational network for the Internet of Value (IoV). The IoV represents a connected and value-centric counterpart to the internet, where the transfer of value is as immediate and seamless as the exchange of information. RippleNet's principles of real-time settlement, interoperability, and decentralization position it as a pioneering force in realizing the IoV.

True Real-Time Settlement Across Ledgers: A pivotal waypoint on the roadmap is the achievement of true real-time settlement across ledgers. Traditional financial systems often grapple with settlement delays and inconsistencies between ledgers. RippleNet's decentralized approach, coupled with the efficiency of XRP, addresses these challenges by enabling true real-time settlement. This milestone not only enhances the speed of cross-border transactions but also serves as a foundation for a synchronized global financial ecosystem.

Unleashing Unforeseen Applications:

Dynamic Nature of Technological Evolution: The roadmap acknowledges the dynamic and unpredictable nature of technological evolution. As we anticipate the future, it is essential to recognize that the evolution of RippleNet and XRP may give rise to applications and use cases that are not yet envisioned. The dynamic nature of technological evolution opens the door to unforeseen innovations that may redefine the landscape of global finance.

Conclusion: Navigating the Future with Confidence

In conclusion, the roadmap to the future of value transfer is a dynamic and multifaceted journey, marked by innovation, collaboration, and a commitment to principles that redefine the financial landscape. RippleNet and XRP, as trailblazers in this journey, continue to evolve, adapt, and expand their capabilities to meet the challenges and opportunities that lie ahead.

As the roadmap unfolds, the collaborative efforts of stakeholders, the foresight of innovators, and the adaptability to emerging trends will be pivotal. The narrative of RippleNet's evolution is an open chapter, with each phase contributing to the broader story of a decentralized, efficient, and inclusive future for global finance. The principles outlined in this roadmap provide a compass for navigating this transformative journey with confidence and purpose, shaping a future where the transfer of value is not only efficient but also an empowering force for individuals and economies worldwide.

THE END

Glossary

Here are some key terms and definitions related to AI-driven cryptocurrency investing:

1. RippleNet: A decentralized network developed by Ripple that connects global payment providers, enabling seamless and standardized cross-border transactions.

2. XRP: The native digital currency of the Ripple network, used as a bridge currency for on-demand liquidity and facilitating real-time settlement across different currencies.

3. Cross-Border Payments: Financial transactions involving the transfer of money or assets between individuals, businesses, or financial institutions across different countries.

4. Digital Assets: Cryptographic representations of value stored and transacted electronically, encompassing cryptocurrencies like XRP, tokens, and other blockchain-based assets.

5. Decentralized Finance (DeFi): A financial ecosystem built on blockchain technology, allowing for decentralized and automated financial services such as lending, trading, and smart contracts.

6. Blockchain Technology: A distributed ledger technology that records transactions across a network of computers, ensuring transparency, security, and immutability.

7. On-Demand Liquidity: The ability to instantly convert one currency to another using a digital asset like XRP, reducing the need for pre-funded accounts and minimizing transaction costs.

8. Smart Contracts: Self-executing contracts with coded terms and conditions that automatically execute and enforce contractual agreements when predefined conditions are met.

9. Internet of Value (IoV): An interconnected and value-centric counterpart to the internet, where the transfer of value is as immediate and seamless as the exchange of information.

10. Interledger Protocol (ILP): An open protocol facilitating payments across different ledgers and networks, providing interoperability and enabling seamless value transfer.

11. Real-Time Settlement: The immediate and final transfer of funds or assets between parties, eliminating delays associated with traditional settlement processes.

12. Standardized Technology and Rules: Consistent protocols and guidelines within RippleNet to ensure uniformity and efficiency in cross-border transactions.

13. API (Application Programming Interface): A set of rules that allows different software applications to communicate with each other, enabling easy integration of business applications with RippleNet.

14. Financial Inclusion: Efforts to provide access to affordable and accessible financial services to underserved and unbanked populations, potentially facilitated by RippleNet.

15. Tokenized Assets: Digitally represented assets on a blockchain, often facilitating the fractional ownership and transfer of real-world assets.

16. Central Bank Digital Currency (CBDC): Digital currency issued by a central bank, representing a digital form of a country's official currency.

17. Supply Chain Finance: The use of financial instruments and technology to optimize and streamline the financing of transactions within a supply chain.

18. Programmable Swaps, Loans, and Escrows: Customizable and automated financial contracts executed on a blockchain, allowing for programmable and conditional execution of financial agreements.

19. Sustainability in Blockchain Operations: Adhering to eco-friendly practices in the operation of blockchain networks, addressing concerns about the environmental impact of blockchain technology.

20. Roadmap: A strategic plan outlining the key milestones, initiatives, and objectives guiding the future development and evolution of RippleNet and XRP.

Potential References

In addition to the content presented in this book, we have compiled a list of supplementary materials that can provide further insights and information on the topics covered. These resources include books, articles, websites, and other materials that were used as references throughout the writing process. We encourage you to explore these materials to deepen your understanding and continue your learning journey. Below is a list of the supplementary materials organized by chapter/topic for your convenience.

Introduction:

Swartz, N. (2019). The Age of Cryptocurrency: How Bitcoin and Digital Money are Challenging the Global Economic Order. St. Martin's Press.

Tapscott, D., & Tapscott, A. (2016). Blockchain revolution: how the technology behind bitcoin is changing money, business, and the world. Penguin.

Chapter 1: RippleNet - A Network of Networks:

Ripple. (2022). RippleNet Overview. https://ripple.com/ripplenet/

Tapscott, D., & Tapscott, A. (2016). Blockchain revolution: how the technology behind bitcoin is changing money, business, and the world. Penguin.

Chapter 2: xRapid - Leveraging XRP for Liquidity:

Ripple. (2022). xRapid: On-Demand Liquidity. https://ripple.com/xrp/on-demand-liquidity/

Ripple Insights. (2018). Unlocking Real Value with XRP. https://ripple.com/insights/unlocking-real-value-with-xrp/

Chapter 3: xCurrent - Interledger for Payment Tracking:

Ripple. (2022). xCurrent: Interledger for Secure Cross-Border Transactions. https://ripple.com/xrp/xcurrent/

20. Roadmap: A strategic plan outlining the key milestones, initiatives, and objectives guiding the future development and evolution of RippleNet and XRP.

Potential References

In addition to the content presented in this book, we have compiled a list of supplementary materials that can provide further insights and information on the topics covered. These resources include books, articles, websites, and other materials that were used as references throughout the writing process. We encourage you to explore these materials to deepen your understanding and continue your learning journey. Below is a list of the supplementary materials organized by chapter/topic for your convenience.

Introduction:

Swartz, N. (2019). The Age of Cryptocurrency: How Bitcoin and Digital Money are Challenging the Global Economic Order. St. Martin's Press.

Tapscott, D., & Tapscott, A. (2016). Blockchain revolution: how the technology behind bitcoin is changing money, business, and the world. Penguin.

Chapter 1: RippleNet - A Network of Networks:

Ripple. (2022). RippleNet Overview. https://ripple.com/ripplenet/

Tapscott, D., & Tapscott, A. (2016). Blockchain revolution: how the technology behind bitcoin is changing money, business, and the world. Penguin.

Chapter 2: xRapid - Leveraging XRP for Liquidity:

Ripple. (2022). xRapid: On-Demand Liquidity. https://ripple.com/xrp/on-demand-liquidity/

Ripple Insights. (2018). Unlocking Real Value with XRP. https://ripple.com/insights/unlocking-real-value-with-xrp/

Chapter 3: xCurrent - Interledger for Payment Tracking:

Ripple. (2022). xCurrent: Interledger for Secure Cross-Border Transactions. https://ripple.com/xrp/xcurrent/

Ripple Insights. (2017). Bringing Interledger to the Enterprise. https://ripple.com/insights/bringing-interledger-to-the-enterprise/

Chapter 4: xVia - A Standard API for Payments:

Ripple. (2022). xVia: A Standard API for Global Payments. https://ripple.com/xrp/xvia/

Ripple Insights. (2017). xVia: A New Way to Pay. https://ripple.com/insights/xvia-a-new-way-to-pay/

Chapter 5: Use Cases - RippleNet in the Real World:

Santander Group. (2022). Santander One Pay FX. https://www.santander.com/en/onepayfx

MoneyGram. (2022). Ripple and MoneyGram. https://corporate.moneygram.com/newsroom/moneygram-and-ripple

MercuryFX. (2022). MercuryFX Transfers Payments in Minutes with Ripple. https://mercury-fx.com

Chapter 6: Beyond Payments - Smart Contracts and NFTs:

Mougayar, W. (2016). The Business Blockchain: Promise, Practice, and Application of the Next Internet Technology. John Wiley & Sons.

Buterin, V., & Mihai, A. (2014). Ethereum: A Next-Generation Smart Contract and Decentralized Application Platform. https://ethereum.org/en/whitepaper/

Chapter 7: The Future with the Internet of Value:

Ripple Insights. (2018). The Internet of Value: What It Means and How It Benefits Everyone. https://ripple.com/insights/the-internet-of-value-what-it-means-and-how-it-benefits-everyone/

Schwartz, N. (2020). An Overview of the Ripple Consensus Algorithm. https://arxiv.org/abs/2004.01605

Conclusion:

Narayanan, A., Bonneau, J., Felten, E., Miller, A., & Goldfeder, S. (2016). Bitcoin and Cryptocurrency Technologies: A Comprehensive Introduction. Princeton University Press.

Ripple. (2022). RippleNet and XRP: A Roadmap to the Future. https://ripple.com/insights/ripplenet-and-xrp-a-roadmap-to-the-future/

www.ingramcontent.com/pod-product-compliance
Lightning Source LLC
LaVergne TN
LVHW012044070526
838202LV00056B/5589